LEVEL UP

ALSO BY STACEY ABRAMS

While Justice Sleeps

Our Time Is Now

Lead from the Outside

Stacey's Extraordinary Words
(with Kitt Thomas)

ALSO BY HEATHER CABOT

The New Chardonnay

Geek Girl Rising
(with Samantha Walravens)

LEVEL UP

·
·
·

RISE ABOVE THE
HIDDEN FORCES HOLDING
YOUR BUSINESS BACK

Stacey Abrams and **Lara Hodgson**

WITH HEATHER CABOT

PORTFOLIO · PENGUIN

PORTFOLIO / PENGUIN
An imprint of Penguin Random House LLC
penguinrandomhouse.com

Most Portfolio books are available at a discount when purchased in quantity for sales promotions or
corporate use. Special editions, which include personalized covers, excerpts, and corporate imprints,
can be created when purchased in large quantities. For more information, please call (212) 572-2232
or e-mail specialmarkets@penguinrandomhouse.com. Your local bookstore can also assist with
discounted bulk purchases using the Penguin Random House corporate Business-to-Business
program. For assistance in locating a participating retailer, e-mail B2B@penguinrandomhouse.com.

Library of Congress Cataloging-in-Publication Data

Names: Abrams, Stacey, author. |
Hodgson, Lara, author. | Cabot, Heather, author.
Title: Level up : rise above the hidden forces holding your business back /
Stacey Abrams and Lara Hodgson, with Heather Cabot.
Description: New York, NY : Portfolio/ Penguin, [2022] |
Includes bibliographical references.
Identifiers: LCCN 2021055166 (print) | LCCN 2021055167 (ebook) |
ISBN 9780593539828 (hardcover) | ISBN 9780593539835 (ebook)
Subjects: LCSH: Small business—Growth. |
Success in business. | Entrepreneurship.
Classification: LCC HD62.7 .A254 2022 (print) | LCC HD62.7 (ebook) |
DDC 658.4/21—dc23/eng/20211117
LC record available at https://lccn.loc.gov/2021055166
LC ebook record available at https://lccn.loc.gov/2021055167

Printed in the United States of America
1   3   5   7   9   10   8   6   4   2

BOOK DESIGN BY MEIGHAN CAVANAUGH

To my parents, Carolyn and Robert Abrams;
my siblings, Andrea, Leslie, Richard, Walter, and Jeanine;
and my nephews and nieces, Jorden, Faith, Cameron,
Riyan, Ayren, and Devin—with love to all.

—STACEY

To Casey, who is the wind beneath my wings.
To Connor, who inspires me daily to personally
Level Up—you are amazing!
To my parents, John and Beverly, who have always
supported my crazy ideas even if they shut down
my first business so I could do homework.
To my sister, Becky, who is gifted in every way that I am not.
To my in-laws, Thom and Grace, for expanding my horizons.
To Cal and Amy and to my nephews, Sonny, Asher, Drew,
Caleb, and Sam, who raise the bar and pay it forward.

—LARA

CONTENTS

•
•
•

PROLOGUE

The moment our business fell apart, we didn't know it was the end.

Like a cruel joke, the wheels began to come off the very day we scored our most important win. On a glorious morning in the fall of 2010, Lara got word that a global retailer wanted to buy fifteen hundred units—twenty times our typical order—of the product we had invented to help busy parents feed their babies. Our patented spill-proof water bottles for little ones were already selling out in small boutiques and on Amazon, but now they would be distributed by a big-time grocery chain. The deal would take Nourish, our scrappy little company, to the next level.

As business partners with varying degrees of risk tolerance, we often jokingly refer to each other as "Yes" and "But." Lara plays the eternal optimist. She's a cheerleader at heart, with a sharp eye for business and a head for innovation, who sees the possibilities in every opportunity. Stacey, on the other hand, serves as the resident realist of our partnership, a cautious contrarian who is a stickler for thoughtful deliberation before we make any big moves. So of course, as soon as she shared word of this news, Lara was ready to go for it while Stacey wondered if we could actually deliver on this opportunity.

But after her initial elation (including a few fist bumps to herself), realization hit Lara hard as she began to think through what it would take to capitalize on the opportunity to truly go national. As she sat in her car in the parking lot of her son's day care, she put her head on the steering wheel and quietly burst into tears. By the time we met to discuss it in our midtown Atlanta office, despair had set in.

To take advantage of this order, we would need to automate our equipment—a big capital investment. And we'd have to pay all our suppliers—another significant outlay. Separately, we'd both reached the same conclusion: We couldn't afford to fulfill the order without payment up front. But the retailer wanted favorable payment terms, granting them thirty days to pay us after we shipped the fifteen hundred bottles. Known as net 30, the arrangement could only work if we had the cash on hand needed to pay our manufacturers to produce the bottles and their labels; to pay our suppliers for the boxes, the brand tags, and the cap safety seals; and to pay to ship the product. All these suppliers and vendors needed to be compensated so they could pay their own suppliers and employees, and, of course, we had to pay our employees. While we had modest revenue, we had not yet turned a profit, which meant we had to wait for retail customers to pay for the orders we'd shipped weeks ago in order to have the money to finance this big break.

Over the next few months, we scrambled to bargain with suppliers who hadn't been paid yet for our previous factory runs. We called everyone we knew, hoping to find another vendor who might do it on credit. We groveled for more time, and we begged customers to pay their invoices. We were able to pull off the first few orders by scrapping and scraping, working in the filling plant ourselves and leaning on the grace of our partners. In the end, six months later, we had to face the painful truth: we just didn't have the cash to pay our vendors to make the product and deliver the new order in the required time frame.

When we launched Nourish, we had cobbled together nearly a quarter of a million dollars from family and friends to produce our water, pitch our merchandise, and set up our company. Any revenue we earned was solely earmarked for the business, plowing the funds back into production, sales, and marketing. But as our customer base grew, they took longer and longer to pay; we were running out of cash while we waited for unpaid invoices to be settled. The hunt for new investors also stalled in a time of tech-focused venture capitalists. No one saw Nourish as the next big thing.

We huddled together in the cramped back office where boxes of samples lined the wall. The brightly lit room had become Stacey's space, the desktop computer where she kept track of outstanding payables and revised pitch decks to investors whirring on the table. Along the walls, built-in shelves had been repurposed as a filing system and storage space for our promotional items. Lime green, our signature color, popped out in random spots around the room—from silk ribbons to random sippy tops to our sales T-shirts.

Lara had returned from meeting with another possible investor. This one was a woman who seemed to get our story and our potential. We'd updated our "cap table," the formal list of our existing shareholders, and produced spreadsheets tracking our growing customer base. Our trajectory, like most small businesses, showed impressive but gradual improvement over time, not the overnight rags-to-riches fables that tantalized most investors. We'd adjusted our expectations of how much equity we would hold if she came on board—knowing that we'd rather have a percentage of something than 100 percent of zero.

But the news wasn't good. Surrounded by our creative flourishes, the cheery color seemed to mock us. The investor was impressed with our business, our projections, and our opportunities, but she'd decided to hold off for the time being. We couldn't guarantee high-enough returns fast enough. She and her firm would not be supplying the cash that would let us reach profitability—cash we would guarantee to repay with regular orders to major retailers, like the order we had on hand.

To fund our dreams, we had used most of the capital sources available in the midst of the Great Recession: a local bank, a credit union, and eventually, a factor, a company that would purchase the unpaid invoices from us at a discount, paying us 80 to 90 percent, and charge us high fees and interest until our customers paid the invoices. But even factoring wasn't foolproof, despite our forecast of customers and future payment. With the financial crisis still reverberating, the factor's credit-scoring model changed, leaving us in the lurch again.

By May 2011, the two of us would make the heart-wrenching decision to let the opportunity go, and with it Nourish, the company we had built from scratch. It would take a few more years for Nourish to finally go under, but our dream of growing died the day our biggest order arrived.

But as much as the failure stung, it would prove to be our greatest lesson. We realized we had actually **grown our company out of business**. It all came down to cash flow and leverage—neither of which we had. We knew there had to be a better way for businesses to get paid, a better way for business owners to manage cash flow, and a better way for small businesses to achieve their potential. We made it our mission to figure out how to help small-business owners like us change the game and LEVEL UP.

1

UNLIKELY BUSINESS PARTNERS

It's Time to Level Up

We decided to write this book because our story is *your* story. Our journey typifies the optimism of entrepreneurship as well as the systemic hurdles challenging small businesses more than ever. To launch a business is to be passionate about fearlessly and independently solving a problem. It's a uniquely American endeavor that has enabled transformative innovation and prosperity. But the promise of business ownership as a ticket to a better life no longer looks as bright as it once did. Despite a record uptick in new business filings during the recovery from the COVID-19 pandemic, entrepreneurship has been on a troubling downward slide for years. The rate of startup creation across the nation plummeted 44 percent between 1978 and 2012, prompting small-business advocates to sound alarms.

Pundits often point to the bleak statistic that half of new businesses do not survive five years. We believe the larger problem is the number of businesses that *stay alive* but just barely, unable to scale to the point of sustainability. These business owners work harder and harder to grow, only to find that "small" is a permanent status. But you wouldn't know it from the sky-high ratings for TV shows like ABC's *Shark Tank* and the breathless media coverage of Silicon Valley unicorns hatched by young hackers. Turns out those high-tech, high-growth tech startups that grab so many headlines actually make up just 1 percent of all new businesses.

For the rest of us, it has never been harder to grow and thrive. As soon as a firm gets a chance to rev up production, close a deal with that dream account, or finally hire people to take on more work, there often isn't enough fuel in the tank to propel it upward. Instead, the opportunity to grow becomes an existential threat, challenging even the most optimistic entrepreneur. Businesses in this position teeter on a razor's edge between living to fight another day or running out of steam and calling it quits. As someone once said to us, the key to entrepreneurship is staying alive long enough to get lucky.

But it shouldn't come down to luck when we know that the most basic need of a small business is access to capital. Capital is how you make your product, how you get your customers, how you tell your story, how you pay your employees. And yet, especially for minority and female-led enterprises, securing that propellant is exceedingly difficult. Minority-owned firms are more likely to be denied bank loans and to pay higher interest rates for credit, and less likely to apply for loans because they rightfully fear they will be denied. At the same time, women-owned ventures account for just 16 percent of conventional small-business loans and 17 percent of SBA loans, even though female-owned firms make up a third of all small companies in the U.S.

Big banks have pulled up stakes in poor and rural communities over the last several decades, so they no longer have a personal connection to business owners and local banks struggling to stay afloat. Compounding the problem is a broken definition: The federal government still considers all firms with fewer than five hundred employees "small" businesses. This broad and outdated catchall lumps together the corner pizza shop, the solo digital-marketing consultant, the general contractor bidding on multimillion dollar government transit projects, and the co-packer with hundreds of workers on an assembly line. When lenders don't consider the unique circumstances and backgrounds of individual business owners, it filters down into loan applications and credit scoring. Banks assume small businesses are miniature large businesses and evaluate them as unfavorable when they don't have the same type of collateral and cash flow as more mature businesses. Right now, the small-business lending division of a large bank looks at a truly small business that is new or being bootstrapped by an underrepresented owner, then compares that operation to an entity with five hundred employees. If the bank's division, which should know better, holds them to the same standard, then of course the real small business will fail in comparison and not be able to qualify for a loan.

Furthermore, disparities between Black and white wealth and the nation's history of redlining means it's far less likely a Black entrepreneur owns a home to use as collateral for a commercial bank loan. For this reason, many Black business owners cannot access loans from traditional lending institutions and often turn to credit cards, their own savings, or nonprofit community lenders.

The COVID-19 pandemic exposed this inequity and misunderstanding by policy makers. Paycheck Protection Program (PPP) loans meant to help small businesses were administered by traditional banks and quickly snapped up by large and established enterprises. This critical fumble by Congress and the Small Business Administration put many marginalized companies on the brink of closure and some out of business for good. Only 12 percent of Black and Latino business owners who said they applied for federal loans in the spring of 2020 received aid. Forty-five percent of Black and Latinx small-business owners who were still in business in May 2020 reported they would have to close by the end of the year, if not sooner.

When it comes to finding investors as a source of capital, it's no secret that women and other marginalized founders encounter more bias and more obstacles than white men—and it's already exceedingly difficult to secure venture capital. It's so tough for most entrepreneurs to access capital that 83 percent of entrepreneurs don't even use bank loans or VC when starting a business. They dip into retirement savings, run up credit card debt, or ramp up slowly while juggling their day jobs.

Then there is the issue of the cash small businesses *lend to* their biggest customers. Yes, you read that right. Lend to, not borrow from. You may not realize it, but small firms are collectively the largest lenders in the U.S. because of the payment terms large corporations and government agencies require. As small companies wait thirty, sixty, or one hundred twenty-plus days for customers to pay invoices, we hold more than $1.2 trillion of trade credit—essentially *loans* we make to our corporate customers *for free*. Small businesses can charge interest, but the large company that's on the hook typically won't pay it. In a monetary battle between David and Goliath, Goliath wins. Large customers being invoiced by a small business have all the power in the relationship, so they can pay late and still take discounts and not pay interest. Demanding net 30 terms means the more financially liquid customer gets thirty days to pay, and they enjoy thirty days of free credit at the cash-strapped small business's expense. Small businesses are treated like indentured lenders to corporate America and public institutions. Small businesses fund the bulk of the economy, and yet they're told to fund our wealthier counterparts, wait to be paid, and like it.

Further, access to marketplaces has been severely limited since the 1980s as antitrust regulations meant to guard against monopolies and to spur competition have steadily eroded, enabling the rise of giants that dominate entire industries. Big Tech has thrown up even more barriers to entry. Companies like Google, Facebook, Apple, and Amazon can control how small firms and creators reach customers in the new algorithm-powered world of targeted consumer advertising. While these behemoths have attempted to respond to the power imbalance, their business models are not designed for anyone's success but their own.

Small businesses have been fighting an uphill battle for decades just to access commerce. These roadblocks keep small businesses small or struggling to grow. It is time to shift the power dynamic for all small businesses, and in *Level Up* we will show you how we can do it together.

It all starts with our story, when the stars aligned to connect two Southern women with very distinct leadership styles and personalities from wholly different upbringings. We improbably joined forces in 2006, and we have founded and grown two multimillion-dollar enterprises. When we stumbled, we conceived of an innovative way to solve the problem that defeated our company. We created a fintech startup called Now Corp, which helps small businesses across the U.S. get paid faster. Now Corp has accelerated close to $1 billion in invoice payments to small firms. The idea was born out of the cash-flow challenges we and others experienced and ignited our desire to change the game.

In *Level Up* we share the story of our fifteen-year journey together. Along the way, we've faced hurdles that were far larger and more powerful than we had imagined. We alone cannot overcome the structures that dictate access to capital and commerce. Yet that revelation should not stop us. To rise above these obstacles, we must start talking about them with one another, with policy makers, and with decision makers. Hundreds of groups have been organized to help small-business owners, and they each have a perspective that matters. But too often, the most broken parts of the system make our challenges look like personal failures, and we rarely discuss those. To galvanize other small-business owners and stakeholders across the entrepreneurial ecosystem, we must tell our stories and deconstruct impediments that are built to keep us outside looking in on growth.

A dizzying array of financial, political, and regulatory systems put small-business owners at the mercy of big banks, corporate America, and Silicon Valley startup worship. Bottom line: It's not you, it's them. So we want to help you better understand the often invisible and unexpected forces that hold back many small firms from fulfilling their potential. Through LEVEL-UP lessons in each chapter, we want what we've learned to be of use to you as your own struggles are reflected in our story. Together, we can expand opportunity in the greatest engine of job creation in this country: America's thirty million small-business owners.

The truth is, neither one of us aspired to become an entrepreneur. In fact, many of you reading this book may not even realize that the Stacey Abrams you see on TV fighting for voting rights quietly cofounded multiple companies when she wasn't campaigning for office or debating bills in Georgia's House of Representatives . . . or dreaming up dramatic new twists in her bestselling novels. And Lara, as a trained rocket scientist—yes, an aerospace engineer— has sold sneakers, built skyscrapers, and raised a family. Like many of you, we joined each other on this unlikely path of small-business ownership at a time when each of us was searching for an avenue to earn a living that would provide a new measure of self-determination and freedom.

Difference Is Our Superpower

Starting a business wasn't even on our minds when we first met in the summer of 2003. We had each been selected to participate in Leadership Atlanta, a rigorous development program that brings together eighty civic, business, and faith leaders to strengthen community ties and address social and economic issues facing the region. We were two of the youngest participants in this esteemed group, which is selected annually by nomination and represents the sweeping diversity of the metro area.

At the time, Stacey, a tax attorney trained at Yale Law School with a master's in public policy from the University of Texas at Austin, was working as Atlanta deputy city attorney after a stint at a big corporate law firm. Atlanta had been Stacey's home since her teens. She attended Spelman, the prestigious historically Black women's college, which nurtured her passion for public service and political activism. Lara, a Harvard MBA, was managing Dewberry Capital, an Atlanta commercial real estate firm, where she served as chief operating officer. She had gone to Georgia Tech on a track-and-field scholarship and was one of three women in her entire aerospace engineering class. She never really wanted to become a rocket scientist; she chose the program because she heard it was the hardest to pursue.

Although we lived just a short car ride away from each other and came from tight-knit, churchgoing families, our backgrounds could not have been further apart. Lara had moved to Atlanta from Rochester, New York, when she was five years old and grew up in a conservative, predominantly white suburb and attended Catholic schools. When she wasn't studying, she packed her afternoons with varsity cheerleading practice, student council, and fierce competition at basketball games and track meets.

Her parents had switched Lara to private education when the local public school in Clarkston, Georgia, could no longer offer enough advanced classes to keep up with her inquisitive mind. Tuition was a stretch for her middle-class family, but her dad, an IRS criminal investigator, and mom, a part-time school administrator, made it work. Their thrift even inspired Lara's first enterprise.

When her classmates began wearing hair barrettes embellished with ribbon and multicolored beads, Lara's mom took her to the fabric store to buy materials so they could make their own. The homemade barrettes were such a hit that the other girls clamored to buy them. Then the owner of the fabric store, intrigued by Lara's increasingly large purchases of supplies, asked if she could start selling the barrettes in her shop. Before long, Lara had friends and family pitching in to make the hair accessories. But when the store owner ordered four hundred pairs in college colors for the upcoming football game between rivals University of Georgia and Georgia Tech, Lara's mother responded that the business was now closed because Lara had homework to do. Schoolwork always came first, and she graduated as valedictorian of her St. Pius X High School class.

Stacey too possessed an insatiable appetite for academics. But she tended to stay closer to home. Throughout her childhood, she devoured library books (including the encyclopedia), pursued a love of science and the arts, went to church every Sunday, and always helped watch over her younger siblings. An introvert, she grew up rich in family and faith, but with little in the way of material wealth. Her parents, who had participated in the Civil Rights Movement as teens, often struggled to make ends meet in their predominantly Black, working-class neighborhood in Gulfport, Mississippi. Although they sometimes couldn't pay the electric bill, Stacey's parents always found ways to contribute to the community and expected their children to work right alongside them in service to others. The kids approached these adventures like they were in an episode of the 1970s TV show *The Love Boat*. Firstborn sister, Andrea, was always captain of the ship, in charge of setting sail. Stacey, next in line, handled "finance and logistics," figuring out how to get it all done, while Leslie, the next Abrams sister, was the cruise director, with all her infectious enthusiasm. The three youngest siblings, two brothers and a sister, were the crew, and they generally followed orders.

The Abrams family carried their passion for helping others to Atlanta when Stacey's mom, a college librarian, and her dad, a shipyard laborer, were accepted into the Candler School of Theology at Emory University. They each received the degree of Master of Divinity while Stacey was in high school. A few years later and across town from Lara, Stacey too was named valedictorian of her Georgia high school.

As we matured and moved into early adulthood, our lives continued to revolve around our graduate work, insular families, budding careers, and community service. We probably would never have connected in a meaningful way if we had not landed in the very same meeting room on a muggy Saturday morning in August 2003.

At the Leadership Atlanta workshop on race relations, the moderator invited Stacey to share a secret dream that most people would never have suspected. Typically reserved and still mulling over when she might launch her political career, Stacey gamely revealed to the crowd that she would like to become president of the United States. Sitting across the room, Lara could hardly contain herself. She felt an immediate kinship. Turns out, she too had aspired to run for the White House and was nearly bursting out of her seat to meet another woman who harbored the very same dream—and would say so out loud.

We still laugh over what happened next, because it is the perfect way to illustrate how different we are. As soon as the room broke for lunch, Lara made a beeline for Stacey, and after the briefest introduction, blurted out her life story even though we were basically complete strangers. Stacey was stunned for a moment. But as we sat down at a table and began to talk over lunch, we developed a connection.

You might assume that two type As bold enough to dream about becoming president, and with different political ideologies, would be instant rivals. But in the eight months that followed, our friendship blossomed. As luck would have it, we landed in the very same Leadership Atlanta study group, a smaller cohort who met once a month for daylong seminars observing courthouses, jails, public works projects, and public schools across the city.

For the two of us, the experience was a crash course in what intrigued our heads and our hearts. We got to see each other be vulnerable and uncomfortable. We got to see each other learn. And we got to see each other pursue a passion to reform part of the state's foster-care system through the community service project our team spearheaded. Our work cemented our mutual respect. We saw how we could leverage our unique perspectives to innovate and help others. We learned that difference was our superpower.

Unexpected Business Owners

As the year went on, our monthly working groups led to more casual meetups one-on-one and, eventually, late-night emailing sessions during which we would ping each other about all the big ideas and plans that kept our minds buzzing when everyone else was asleep. One of the things we discovered about each other is that we are both night owls. We get our best thinking done at 2:00 a.m. And the one idea we couldn't stop thinking about was one day finding a way to work together. By December 2006, the time was right.

We didn't even call ourselves entrepreneurs at first. In our minds, that was a title reserved for coders in hoodies in garages out in Menlo Park. We were just two highly ambitious friends who had reached a stage in our lives when working for someone else no longer fit our goals. By this point, Stacey had decided to run for her first elected office, a seat in the Georgia House of Representatives. If she won, she would need to find a more flexible way to supplement the $17,310 part-time salary she would earn as a politician. As soon as she announced her candidacy in 2005 for the 2006 Democratic Primary, Stacey stepped down from her municipal post and started Sage Works, a private consultancy. If elected, she would be voting on matters that involved the city of Atlanta and wanted to avoid potential conflicts of interest. Stacey won her election and had landed a few clients, but she did not enjoy the hunt for new business. Over the next year, she repeatedly turned to Lara for advice on how to leverage her proven skills to find more projects.

Lara was running one of Atlanta's largest commercial real estate firms and had just been appointed by Republican governor Sonny Perdue to serve on the Transit Planning Board. She was also about to become a mom and wanted more flexibility in her schedule. As we discussed our concerns and potential choices by the nighttime glow of our laptops, we finally decided the only solution would be to go into business together, drawing on our respective expertise, and essentially designing the jobs we wanted for ourselves on our own terms. And so, in the middle of the night at the end of a tumultuous year, Insomnia Consulting, our very first enterprise together, came to be.

The way we started our business is the story of American entrepreneurship. Eighty-one percent of small businesses in the U.S. are owned by sole proprietors. They, like us, are people who took the leap to become their own bosses, to hang out a shingle in hopes of generating a reliable income and having more control over their time. In reality, most entrepreneurs create the job they wish they had before ever thinking about building a whole company.

During the economic recovery from the COVID-19 pandemic, the highest number of Americans since 2004 made the very same calculation either by necessity or by choice. They turned side hustles into new careers, leveraging untapped skills in the face of layoffs and shuttered businesses and parlaying their ingenuity and drive into moneymaking ventures. Through May 2021, a record number of marketers, interior designers, nutritionists, attorneys, painters, caterers, jewelry designers, electricians, accountants . . . you name it, asked the IRS for new federal tax ID numbers so they could start doing business. The 24.3 percent surge in new filings in 2020 and beyond drew a stark contrast to the landscape following the Great Recession, where new business formations lagged in the wake of the Lehman Brothers crash. According to University of Maryland economist John Haltiwanger and his colleagues, the majority of new firms emerging today, as opposed to after the 2008 financial crisis, are owned by solopreneurs. What remains to be seen is whether those new businesses will ever reach the point when they expand to create new jobs and whether they continue in business after the founder has stopped working.

This is a central question we encountered when we started Insomnia Consulting. The challenge is to define whether what you have created is a "lifestyle" business for yourself or, potentially, something much bigger that can sustain itself without your running the show 24/7. You have to ask yourself whether you want to build a company or whether you simply want to work for yourself. Lifestyle businesses are vital and a core of the small-business universe, but they're not what we're writing about here. We had both come from families that worked for others, and we both dreamed of businesses that could make money while we slept (when we managed to). These sustainable enterprises that become generational wealth vehicles require a different mindset and face distinct obstacles. The first of which is knowing which type of company you intend to build.

If you think you are ready to hire employees so you can take on more customers in hopes of growing profits exponentially and build an entity that is able to flourish independent of you personally, that is a very different road from solopreneurship. Leveling up is about reaching that critical moment of lift—that moment when you hit an inflection point of growth that means your company can grow without limits. We will take you along for the ride as we made our own decisions about our business future, at Insomnia and beyond, and we'll introduce you to some other inspiring entrepreneurs we met along the way.

One thing we know for sure is that when you are doing something you have never done before, having a partner who shares your vision and your values but has a completely different perspective on how to get it done is not only exciting, it is essential. And it all started with insomnia—and the decision to take a risk on each other to see where and how far we could go.

LEVEL-UP LESSONS:
CHAPTER 1

- Entrepreneurship can be a plan or it can be a necessity. Follow your own path. Don't compare yourself to others.

- Diverse thinking leads to fresh ideas. Seek it out. Look at your team: If everyone looks alike, speaks alike, thinks alike, and believes the same things as you, your team is not diverse.

- Differences can be your superpower. Stay different! Many companies hire people who are diverse thinkers, then train everyone to think the same way. Resist this urge.

- Dig deeper to find root causes or systemic issues rather than solving for symptoms. It will spark greater innovation.

- Acknowledge hurdles and forces that are bigger than you, but don't let that deter you. Instead, find others to help you tilt the scales in your favor.

2

. . .

WATCH OUT FOR
GRIZZLIES

As the cargo plane descended onto a narrow airstrip, we looked out the window with trepidation and wonder. Underneath us was the vast Arctic Sea and the craggy coastline thick with evergreens as far as the eye could see. A year into working together at our firm Insomnia Consulting, we hit the road to meet all kinds of clients. But landing twenty-six miles north of the Arctic Circle in the season when the sun never sets was our most far-flung adventure yet. Here we were, two Southern ladies—and Stacey, who grew up in coastal Mississippi, was adamant she "didn't do below seventy degrees." We had made the long trek from Atlanta to Kiana, Alaska, population 400, to meet with the tribal elders of the Kobuk River Kowagmiut Iñupiat Eskimos in hopes they would bless our small consulting firm's new contract with the Alaska Native Corporation, known as NANA.

With Stacey's expertise in nonprofit tax law and complex government infrastructure projects, and Lara's deep knowledge of real estate and high finance, NANA wanted our help with its plans to continue to generate reliable dividends from the tribe's wide array of investments and properties, which supported the local Indigenous population and its descendants. The money funded physical infrastructure critical to survival in this distant region.

As soon as we settled in at the Arctic Alaska Kiana Lodge, our hosts, Lorry and Nellie Schuerch, explained that our "meeting" with the NANA executives would begin the next day with an all-day fishing excursion. The following morning, in preparation for the trip, we slipped on heavy, full-body rain gear to guard against the hordes of birdlike mosquitoes buzzing over the wetlands. Instead of schmoozing with NANA executives around a staid conference table, the tribe wanted us to experience life on the water in Kiana and witness the spiritual role nature played in their ancient culture. Although neither of us would call fishing a favorite activity, we put on our game faces and yellow slickers and prepared for a day on the river, hours from civilization.

By the time we arrived at the picturesque spot and were briefed on fishing protocols and techniques, we were confident things were going well. Stacey cast her line into the water and quickly reeled it back. Over and over, she sent the lure skipping over the sun-dappled water, but pulled the bait in before a sheefish could bite. One of the men approached with a kind smile and explained that her technique guaranteed she wouldn't land anything. Stacey replied that she'd grown up fishing and confessed she had no interest in actually catching one to simply let it go. "What point would it prove?" she thought. But out of respect (and pride), she expertly cast again, and soon landed three fish in a row—then hustled out of the freezing water.

When it was time to break for lunch on the boat that had brought us here, though, Lara wouldn't stop fishing. She kept casting her line, reeling in sheefish, then releasing them, notching an impressive number that dazzled our hosts. The men remarked to Stacey, who had gladly returned to the boat after catching her requisite fish, "Wow, your partner's, like, *really* competitive. She won't stop for lunch because she wants to catch the most fish."

While a fair assumption given Lara's competitive spirit, what they didn't realize was that Lara didn't stop fishing because she wanted to catch the most fish. She didn't want to have to use the restroom. You see, our hosts had explained during the morning briefing that grizzly bears roamed the area quite frequently. If we needed to "go," they would need to give us a handgun to protect ourselves, since the only place to heed nature's call was in the woods. Lara decided that abstaining from food and drink was worth it to avoid a possible run-in with a grizzly. She just kept fishing, praying that temporary dehydration would be less painful than the alternative.

Thankfully, we didn't meet any bears that day. But we did win the NANA contract and earned the right to work with the amazing people of NANA. (If you ever get the chance to visit this region of the world, you will not be disappointed in the resilience and kindness of the Iñupiat.) The trip to the top of the world was yet another example of how we each pushed each other out of our comfort zones to build our firm. From the start, the whole idea of being in business for ourselves was as foreign as ending up on a boat in the Alaskan wilderness or worrying about fending off grizzlies.

Everything about running our own business was new to us. Neither of us had ever been entrepreneurs. We didn't come from families of business owners. We liked regular paychecks. If we didn't drum up new clients, we didn't have an income. Our clients expected knowledge we didn't yet possess. The array of issues that swirled around our startup was terrifying and confounding. Like the grizzlies that lurked in the woods, or the sheefish that could be caught but not kept, running a small business is fraught with unexpected challenges and almost-wins. But we figured it out as we went along by leaning on each other when doubts or concerns bubbled up. From the very beginning, a big part of navigating the journey of who did what and how much we each contributed was being unafraid to say what we were thinking. Working together as partners required extreme candor.

Hard Conversations Early and Often

One thing that helped, looking back, was the fact that although we like and respect each other, we are not best friends. We go home to our separate lives, and that distance really keeps most tensions at bay. We also acknowledge freely that we each have an ego. It's one of the reasons we are both successful people. We're used to being the best at what we do. Our egos are fed by finding an answer to a difficult problem, rather than knowing all the answers. We were honest about that from the start. We also had candid conversations about what parts of the business we each enjoyed and what we wanted out of it.

Lara is a natural saleswoman with infectious energy. She will talk to anybody. And even though she studied engineering and has a mathematical brain, there is nothing she hates more than spreadsheets. On the other hand, Stacey, despite her celebrity and political career, is much more comfortable building and running operations behind the scenes rather than pitching clients face-to-face. And she loves to write. We divided up the work according to our unique talents and passions. We made Lara the CEO and Stacey the COO. As we started working on projects like writing a case study for NASA executives taking a course at Georgia Tech, or mapping out plans to redevelop former landfill sites, we continued to refine what we wanted clients to see of our respective roles and how we wanted to present ourselves. But that evolved in real time. It didn't happen overnight, and it wasn't always easy.

Early on, we made a presentation to a group of real estate developers in Houston related to one of our landfill projects. During the pitch, the long table of white men would direct questions only to Lara. She didn't seem to notice they were ignoring Stacey. Lara was in the zone, focusing intently on responding to the prospective clients' inquiries. Every time Stacey tried to chime in, the men would redirect the conversation to Lara, treating her as the "brains" of the operation and Stacey as the assistant. They barely acknowledged Stacey's presence. By the end, she had gone silent, chafing at both their disrespect and the fact that Lara didn't see what was happening. But she didn't confront the room, not wanting to alienate an important potential new source of income.

We drove straight to the airport. Lara gushed about how well the meeting went, replaying all the highlights. We knew this could be one of our biggest clients, and Lara was thrilled. But Stacey was withdrawn as we turned onto the highway. Stacey had been trying to decide how to communicate that she was deeply bothered by what had transpired in the meeting. She knew it was unfair to blame Lara for not being attuned to the subtle cues of racism that Stacey had endured her entire life, like being mistaken for a secretary or a paralegal in her corporate law firm despite her Yale law degree.

Often in partnerships, you blame the other person for not knowing how you feel, or you internalize it until it eats at you. But you need to speak up or it will fester. When Lara asked why she wasn't in a celebratory mood, Stacey knew she had to say something or she would regret it. She took a deep breath and finally laid it out. Lara was shocked that she had missed the signals Stacey had seen so clearly. Stacey said she knew Lara would have noticed if the men's dismissiveness was gender driven but explained that they were demeaning Stacey as a Black woman. One by one, Stacey flagged the precise instances of disregard, and the moments when, if she had been allowed to speak in the meeting, she could have contributed valuable information that would have strengthened the pitch.

We sat silently for a moment. Lara was used to navigating male-dominated spaces and countering sexism by charging right past it. She conceded that her competitive drive had created a blind spot in this case. For the rest of our drive, we reflected on what we could do better to head off these situations in the future. First and foremost, as CEO and COO, we would spell out to prospective clients that we were partners as soon as we walked through the door. And before we dove into a presentation, we would remember always to lead with Stacey's credentials when making introductions. This way, there would be no mistaking our shared authority. It was one of the hardest yet most important conversations we would have as partners. Out of that tense drive, we learned that in order to be successful, we had to be intentional about confronting challenges head-on, even when it would hurt to do so.

The frank discussion set the stage for times Lara needed to clear the air too. When Stacey helped manage the Atlanta mayoral campaign of a friend, she dropped the ball following up on clients with open invoices that needed to be paid. That meant more pressure on Lara to cover for her. Stacey was supposed to check in to make sure Lara could handle the workload as the campaign obligations kicked up. But she didn't, and finally, it all came to a head one day when Lara confessed in frustration that she was completely overwhelmed. There was no other choice but for Stacey to own it and admit she needed to do better. We realized from the get-go that the most important part of our business partnership across every business we've started and across every challenge is that we tell each other the truth. That honesty can be painful, and it can be embarrassing. But if you can't do that, then you can't meet success.

Many of the businesses we've encountered—those run by friends and classmates, clients we have served, firms we have partnered with large and small—often run into trouble when egos and personalities push aside the basic decorum that we all know to maintain: *You don't make the other guy do all the work. You don't take credit for other people's work. You don't say you are going to split the check and then leave someone else with the bill.* Sometimes in the speed and intensity of being in business we lose sight of those fundamentals, and we begin to act like we're in an episode of *Dynasty*. Luckily, we figured this out in the early days. Even when our ideologies and our approach to solving problems diverged, we could always return to the fact that we respected each other deeply and knew that our values aligned.

What helped was putting our "rules of engagement" down in writing, to remind us of our core mission when things got crazy. One afternoon over tea, we pulled out a yellow legal pad and sat down at Lara's dining-room table to hammer them out. One of the first priorities was a "no-assholes" policy. We wouldn't do business with anyone who treated us or those around us poorly. Period. At one point, that meant firing our most lucrative client because his business practices conflicted with our ethical standards. Losing the money hurt, but not as much as falling into the trap of easy money would have.

We decided we would only take on projects that intrigued our "heads **and** our hearts." We had to have passion about the work we took on if we were going to put in the time. Further, we wrote down that we wanted to do "work that changes the world." Both of us naturally think big, and we did not want to spend time and effort if we could not have a measurable impact. To underscore why we had gone out on our own in the first place, to have more freedom and control over our time, we scribbled down and circled a key tenet: "Life comes first." We each acknowledged that our respective responsibilities, like caring for aging parents, children, friends, political aspirations, church, marriage, you name it, would not be allowed to fall to the wayside no matter what. The timeworn adage about business, "it's not personal," never sat well with us. We always believed that business *is* personal, and we still do, today more than ever.

As an entrepreneur, you are selling yourself short if you think you can turn off the elements of your life that exist outside the confines of your business. You can't, and more importantly, doing so cuts off part of what drives you. To be successful, you have to acknowledge those very real pressures on your time and energy and be honest about them. At the same time, we learned that addressing those very pressures led to our best ideas. We vowed we would keep our real lives in the center of our decision making. Finally, since we are two insomniacs, we had to include on our list that "sleep is optional" to remind us never to take ourselves too seriously.

The "rules" became our touchstone as the workload picked up and our outside lives also demanded more of our time. One Christmas, Stacey even surprised Lara with a desk clock engraved with the five principles. It was an important reminder as Insomnia Consulting quickly expanded. We needed the priorities to ground us. We were bringing in over a million dollars in revenue within the first year with almost no overhead. We had no equipment other than our laptops and no office space. We often met in cafés or found space at Georgia Tech or sat at one of our kitchen islands or dining-room tables to brainstorm.

Per our original division of labor, Lara was tasked with "catching" while Stacey was charged with "cooking." Lara, ever the saleswoman, would find the clients and close the deals. Then Stacey would follow up in her mild-mannered yet firm way. She would get the customers to sign the contracts and she would delineate the details of our work. We would do a little spec project for them, but then Stacey would reach out and remind the client that she still needed them to sign the agreement that stated how much they were going to pay Insomnia every month. She would continue to do so until the checks came in. If not, she would be the one to withhold the deliverables.

One thing we never fought over with each other was money. When the revenue came in, we would write checks to each other. We found a way to split the profits fairly based on the roles we fulfilled in the firm. Since Lara was bringing in the customers and Stacey likes nothing less than soliciting new clients, we agreed that Lara would get an extra 15 percent on the prospects she landed. On one occasion, Stacey proudly landed a client—quite by accident—and for the first time qualified for the 15 percent bonus. She was careful never to do it again. The division of labor and the allocation of revenue worked for us and laid the groundwork for the future as our partnership evolved over a decade and a half and our commitments outside the business took shape.

Make Money While You Sleep

It wasn't long before we realized the downside of running a business that relied entirely on our intellectual capital. As we balanced our need to generate new clients with the capacity to deliver stellar work, we learned that you can't outsource your brain. No matter how driven you are, there are only so many hours in a day in which you can operate at 100 percent—even two insomniacs like us. This hit Stacey hard late one night, as she opened up her laptop at the mahogany dining table with the wobbly leg she hadn't had time to tighten. She had reached the point of near exhaustion. The legislature was in session and she had spent the day poring over new House bills covering everything from arcane tax policy reform to horse-food labeling, only to come home and settle in for a long night of writing a case study for a new Insomnia client. She had done all the research herself to master the highly technical topic and was the only one who could synthesize the complex material now splayed across the only surface in her townhouse large enough to accommodate so many documents. She knew she couldn't just phone it in. This was our livelihood. At the same time, the task was pulling on all the parts of her brain she used for other pursuits she cared about, like the creativity she drew on while writing fiction and the analytical precision she relied on while considering new legislation. She kept thinking about how Lara once talked about making money while you sleep, essentially using our intellectual capital to make a product that could sell itself. Nothing sounded more enticing that midnight with a pile of work ahead, when all Stacey wanted to do was grab some shut-eye. She powered through, but the desire to find ways to make money while we slept lingered.

We ultimately hired contractors who could work on pieces of the bigger accounts, but that increasingly put us in the position of managing staff to make sure the output met our standards instead of doing the work we really enjoyed. Our income had never been higher, yet our balance sheet was weak. It was exhausting for Lara to keep looking for new customers and for Stacey to make sure they paid us, in addition to both of us doing the actual consulting work. After a year of this feverish pace, not long after we returned from our Alaska business trip, we hit a crossroads.

Our client base relied heavily on complex infrastructure projects, yet the real estate market and soon the world economy would stutter to a halt. Through Lara's outreach and Stacey's contacts, we had diversified our projects, but the newer jobs demanded more and paid less. Chasing invoices had become a central part of Stacey's function, a far cry from the kind of work that stimulates the mind. And Lara sat in pitch meeting after pitch meeting, articulating what Insomnia could offer despite the mundanity of the work available. We knew we could easily grow the business, despite the economy, and make a good living, but Insomnia's trajectory was not sustainable. Unless we added more consultants, dedicated more time to pursuing clients and chasing late payers, we would be on a treadmill. Multimillion-dollar consulting firms are a gold mine for their owners, and we likely could have joined their ranks. But our axioms for doing business demanded we take a close look at our future. We also had other things pulling on our time—family, politics . . . Something had to give! We had to answer the question: Did we want to keep growing a business that we knew would never survive without the two of us grinding away, or did we want to try to scale to the size of a giant consultancy like McKinsey or Accenture? Or did we want to find a new way to leverage our brain power, so that we could sit back and make money while we slept?

As we shared in chapter 1, most small businesses in the U.S. are owned by sole proprietors. And what we experienced is familiar to those "solopreneurs" who, like us, started a business to create a job for themselves . . . and then got stuck on a hamster wheel when the job takes on a life of its own.

Grow Up or Give Up

It may sound counterintuitive, but sometimes the *perception* of success is a hidden force that can hold your business back. You think that because you have so much work coming in that you've achieved your end goal. *But what if there could be more?* What if you can build something that can live beyond your day-to-day involvement and maybe even your lifetime? Unlocking the next level requires a business owner to think not just about success in terms of today's profits but also in terms of the longevity of the business itself. *Can it survive if you are not around?*

Our friend Sheila Jordan, an Atlanta learning technologist, confronted this question a few years ago. With her firm Knowledge Architects, starting in 2010, she carved out a lucrative niche managing instructional learning for some of the biggest transit systems in America. Her manuals and e-classes teach workers like bus and train mechanics in major cities, including New York, Dallas, and Atlanta, how to repair and maintain rapidly modernizing equipment. The business employs twelve full-time employees and generates $8 million in annual revenue with multiyear contracts across the country.

As Sheila gained more customers, she struggled early on to find and onboard the right contractors to staff projects. She wanted to keep taking new clients but couldn't clone herself to serve them all. As a "one-woman show," she realized the business was growing so fast that she didn't have the right internal processes to manage new hires. It was stressful. But Sheila soldiered on. The daughter of two janitors with little education beyond elementary school, she was the first in her family to earn a college degree. Growing up in the 1960s in Oakland, California, she could only dream of a life beyond her family's crowded apartment, let alone being at the helm of her own multimillion-dollar company. Her mom and dad worked the night shift at a suburban Bank of America, and every afternoon while she did her homework, Sheila also cared for her nine brothers and sisters.

"There weren't a lot of opportunities. There weren't a lot of role models. Out of sheer survival and wanting to just do better . . . it just pushed me outside of my box," Sheila told us, as she reflected on how she persisted, earning college and graduate degrees driven by a desire for a more stable life for herself and, later, her own two daughters.

On the surface, Knowledge Architects seemed to be everything Sheila could ever want. She had leveled up. But only to a point: the business had not broken from the tether of Sheila needing to manage it 24/7. If she decided she was done with consulting, the company would have died. To survive, she would need to think about succession planning, either training someone to take it over or selling the business. Or she could find a way to make money while she slept.

It took a chance conversation over a chicken dinner in 2015 to help her realize she could unleash a whole new level of her business. When a man sitting at her banquet table mentioned his company had worked on a project for General Electric building a 3D model of a train, bells suddenly went off in her head. Sheila realized she could turn her consulting services into an actual product. She was already experimenting with augmented reality and 3D tools. The ability to enable a mechanic to learn on a digital model how to disassemble and rebuild complex pieces of equipment was revolutionary. But what if Knowledge Architects could find a way to develop its own educational software, host the curriculum on its own server, and license it to companies? She could scale her firm in a way she never could as a solo operator by creating an entirely new revenue stream that would not depend on her services alone.

In 2018, she launched AR4Transit, the world's only Content as a Service (CaaS) platform that delivers augmented reality work instructions for the transit industry. She was able to pay for the development of the technology by leveraging the cash flow from her biggest customers. Three of the transit agencies her company was already serving invested $650,000 in a five-year revenue-sharing deal that allowed her to launch a pilot. Eventually, Sheila will seek to raise more outside funding. She knows it will be a challenge given the fact that companies led solely by women raised less than 2.2 percent of venture dollars, or $2.6 billion in the first eight months of 2021, a decline from each of the last five years. And just .034 percent of VC, or $494 million, went to female founders of color, according to data compiled by Crunchbase. But she is charging full speed ahead.

We are not saying that everyone must come up with a brilliant tech startup idea to scale their business. But Sheila's story shows how it's important as a solopreneur to choose whether you want to start a lifestyle business that stops when you stop, or whether you want to own something you can scale. One is not better than the other, but you should consciously decide when you start your business, as opposed to becoming a victim when it's not what you thought it would be. And once you start, if you want to sustain the business and grow it to be more than a "job" for you, you have to think about what that might entail and keep your eyes open for opportunities to productize your service as Knowledge Architects is doing with AR4Transit.

If you decide to build a business that will live on beyond the day you stop working, you have to think differently about investing in the things that will hold or grow in value over time, and your unit of value cannot solely be time. You have to invest in assets that will be valuable to others who acquire the business after you leave it or sell it.

Sheila scaled by productizing her service—that is, turning her service into a product. Another way to build a bigger business is by doing the reverse—turning your product into a service. Call it servitizing. Leasing is one way to "servitize" a product. One of our favorite examples is the story of Interface Carpets and its CEO, Ray C. Anderson, an early sustainability pioneer whose company introduced modular flooring and carpeting to offices. A customer could replace a few squares instead of the whole carpet if a section got stained or damaged. Then, to reduce the company's environmental footprint, he decided to stop selling carpet altogether and instead began selling the *use of carpet.* Interface installs carpet squares, and after several years of use, the company swaps out the old carpet with new squares. The old carpet could be reused (such as squares that had been under tables and never stepped on) or recycled. Instead of selling a product, the company sells the service of using a product.

It was becoming clear to us that we needed to come up with our own new path to sustain our business and our sanity. Insomnia was becoming more than the name of our company; it was becoming our state of being.

By the fall of 2007, we knew that Stacey's work in the legislature in the upcoming session would surely demand more of her time. She was already looking ahead to her next campaign and was also trying to finish writing a romantic suspense novel. Lara was getting involved in public service work of her own while finding her footing as a new mom. We often discussed our futures and the future of Insomnia during one of our most cherished weekly traditions. While many people in business like to play eighteen holes to relax, our version of golf was treating ourselves to high tea on occasional Friday afternoons. Over tiered platters of crustless cucumber-and-cream-cheese sandwiches, scones, clotted cream, and lemon curd, we would sink into the plush couches of posh hotels around town and take a moment to breathe and go over our workload. For two people who love solving puzzles, the conversations inevitably turned to the next code we wanted to crack: *What could we do to make money while we slept?* Little did we know, the answer would reveal itself when we least expected it.

LEVEL-UP LESSONS:
CHAPTER 2

- Successful partnerships require extreme candor more than close friendship. Find the middle ground with someone you can trust but who is not in every facet of your life so you each have space.

- Scaling big ideas requires common mindsets but diverse thinking and skill sets. A great partner will agree on the end goal but not always on the way to get there.

- Starting a business has never been easier but scaling a business has never been harder. Don't give up after the sexy *Shark Tank* part.

- Scaling a professional service business is hard because *you* are the product and your unit of value is time. Neither scale. To make money while you sleep, you will need to acquire other people's time or develop a deliverable not measured by time.

- Look for new revenue streams that allow you to make money while you sleep. If you have a service, think about how you can productize it. If you have a product, think about how you can servitize it. New revenue streams that sell more to existing customers drive engagement and value.

3

. . .

IT'S NOT WHAT YOU KNOW. IT'S WHAT YOU NOTICE.

The lunch rush at Ted's Montana Grill attracted a boisterous, time-crunched crowd stopping in for a fast bison burger or steak. We, too, had planned to squeeze in a quick bite in Buckhead with two of Stacey's college friends and campaign staffers in the fall of 2006. But Lara was running late. When she finally burst through the entrance, toting Connor, her eleven-month-old son, she seemed uncharacteristically flustered. The baby wailed as she gingerly squeezed past the other customers to reach our booth. Lara apologized, setting down the infant carrier and then reaching for a napkin to clean off the baby formula soaking the front of her shift dress. She had spilled Connor's bottle all over herself as she rushed to prepare it while sitting in her parked car outside the restaurant. In exasperation, she wondered aloud to nobody in particular, "Why doesn't someone make spill-proof bottled water to mix formula for babies?"

It was a funny question considering that we lived in Atlanta, in the shadow of Coca-Cola's global headquarters and its massive Dasani bottled-water division. What Lara meant wasn't simply water marketed for babies and little children, but water in a convenient kid-size, no-mess container with a sippy spout or a silicone nipple that parents could just grab and go or use to prepare formula on the go. *Did a product like that exist?* No one at the table had ever heard of anything like it. We stopped and looked at each other. Stacey grinned.

"Maybe *we* should do it," she mused with a glimmer in her eye.

We laughed about it for a minute. The fact was, we had more work than we could handle with our growing consulting firm. By the time we dug into our meal, the conversation shifted to the fast-approaching election and Stacey's inaugural run for the state assembly, and we went on with our lunch date. Lara asked the waiter for a glass of water so she could mix a new bottle for the baby, and once fed, Connor happily quieted down. But the "baby water" idea didn't.

Months later, we were busy as ever with Insomnia client projects, but baby water was still gnawing at us. We wanted to pivot our firm from professional services to something more scalable, and we were on the hunt for opportunities. But could baby water *really* be our next venture? Neither of us knew the first thing about the bottled-water business or the baby products industry. Yet the prospect was tantalizing. If it worked, we would be selling water and earning revenue regardless of our other commitments. A product company would free up Lara to put more time into being a mom and building a company that could scale. And Stacey could help grow the company, write more books, and stand for office without dropping one of the balls . . . Why not give it a shot?

But we truly did not know where to start. All we knew, based on some cursory Google searches and browsing in supermarkets, was that no one had patented this type of product yet. We shared a gut feeling that this could be big if we could figure out how to do it. And of course, we both love tackling problems that seem impossible to solve. Yes, it would be a risk to eventually leave behind the consulting firm, but we would approach this new prospect in our own deliberate manner, following our own rules of engagement. We wouldn't rush into it.

You Don't Have to Love Risk

One of the myths that's been elevated in today's era of sexy tech startups is that to be a true entrepreneur, you must love taking risks. But this perception often keeps many would-be founders from even trying, because they have heard so many times that most startups fail. A 2020 Kauffman Foundation survey of people who came up with a business idea but abandoned it before starting revealed that 49 percent gave up because they didn't believe the business would survive. Fifty-five percent of women quit before they started.

We are not big risk-takers. We are risk neutral, meaning that we protect ourselves from the worst that could happen while still embracing the volatility—and possibility—of entrepreneurship. More important, though, we are very comfortable with *ambiguity*. Risk and ambiguity are quite different ways to think about your prospects. We weren't going to leap off a cliff without a parachute, which is a risk calculation. We ensured that we still had income from our consulting firm and health insurance when we decided to shift into starting another business. We also had serious and real financial obligations: Stacey was taking care of her parents. Lara had a new baby. We were not going to sell everything we had, sign personal guarantees for big loans, gamble everything, and sit in folding chairs in a garage eating ramen noodles to start a company. The truth is, most entrepreneurs don't do that anyway. Most business owners do not risk it all, but they understand their exposure.

Successful founders are even more comfortable with ambiguity: the *uncertainty* of not knowing all the answers, not knowing the next steps. We weren't just okay with the uncertainty, we thrived on it. If you don't know the next step, then you can be curious. You can be open-minded. You can allow an opportunity to come your way. Whereas if you're so anxious to have every next step planned out, then you're not open to opportunities. You're not noticing them.

In our experience, great ideas come from *noticing* a problem. Current startup culture tends to celebrate creating a cool thing, then looking for a problem to solve. That's one way to do it, but seeing a need is not only viable but infinitely valuable. Part of the benefit is giving yourself permission to have an idea that is *not* in your area of expertise. The other advantage comes from using your lack of knowledge and concomitant desire to learn as your strength, not your weakness. We didn't know anything about the water business, but we were sure we had identified a problem worth trying to solve. The quest for answers was the fun part and the lucrative one—if we got it right.

Don't Be Afraid to Share Your Idea

Like most inventors, one of the things we weren't certain about was how to get started without someone stealing our idea. We wanted to keep our new concept under wraps, but that hindered our ability to get it off the ground. Lara turned to a trusted old friend for advice, Spanx founder Sara Blakely. Against the odds, Sara revolutionized the world of women's undergarments with her own patented product. By the time Lara sat down with her for coffee, Spanx had become a household name, thanks to Oprah, and was on its way to becoming a billion-dollar company. At twenty-seven, Sara started selling Spanx out of her Atlanta apartment with nothing more than a fax machine, five thousand dollars in savings, and her irrepressible spunk. She had famously written the Spanx patent application herself seated in the Barnes & Noble on Peachtree Road in Atlanta, which is where she met with Lara one afternoon as we started working on our baby-water idea.

Lara confided what we were trying to do and how we worried that doing market research might give away our idea. Sara stressed we couldn't let that fear hold us back. She was emphatic that if we wanted to get this off the ground, we needed to tell people, especially moms, our target audience, precisely so we could get their input. She was obsessed with customer feedback, because scrappy startups can't afford to pay for customer research. Sara gave us a key piece of guidance that proved pivotal: If you *don't* share it, how is anyone going to help? Most people are too busy to take your idea, she said, so we should focus our energy on getting it out into the market and to customers.

So we started sharing. But as Sara also advised, we asked everyone to sign nondisclosure agreements—even, to his surprise, Lara's husband, Casey, then an executive at Coca-Cola. He thought we were kidding until he looked at Stacey and she assured him we were not. We wanted Casey to introduce us to a high-level executive at Dasani who might want to license this big idea from us. We thought we needed a partner to make it a reality; we weren't planning to manufacture the products ourselves. But when the meeting didn't materialize as quickly as Lara hoped, she asked Casey for another contact. He connected us to a retired bottling executive named Mike McNally, who agreed to let us take him to lunch.

It was Mike who inspired us to think bigger. He thought we should try to do this ourselves and offered to introduce us to the owner of a natural water spring in Dandridge, Tennessee, so we could begin to understand the water-bottling business and all it entailed.

A few days later, we set off on a four-hour road trip to the foot of the Great Smoky Mountains to meet the owner of English Mountain Spring Water Company. John Burleson's friendly Southern accent endeared him to us immediately. He graciously led us on a walking tour of English Mountain's large bottling plant. Surrounded by thick forest with a burbling mountain creek running behind the property, the setting could not have been more picturesque. The two freshwater springs situated just nine hundred feet from the plant sparkled with possibility.

As we waved hello to his employees working on the assembly line, John led us around. We carried spiral notebooks and scribbled furiously as he talked. We became students, peppering John with dozens of questions, which he patiently answered. We wanted to know how he measured the water quality. We wanted to understand the difference between spring water and purified water. When we finally described our baby-water vision to John, he said we needed to start thinking about how to package it.

We had a unique logo developed by Stacey's college friend Damon Avent. He designed a logo and bottle shape that evoked the comfort and care we wanted our users to feel. Though he wasn't a graphic designer, he worked with us on colors and shapes until we had the look and feel that told our story. But John's question remained: What would the actual bottles look like?

This question led us to Matt Hughes, who had worked for Jones Soda Co. and was working with a startup water company called Flo. His son was eventually Lara's son's preschool classmate. He and Lara met for coffee, and Matt introduced us to Scott Curlee, whose family owned an Atlanta packaging company called Inmark. Scott would become a dear friend, and Stacey even named a character after him in her legal thriller, *While Justice Sleeps.* Scott guided us through the intricate process of designing the Nourish bottles. He helped us find the right preform, the plastic tubes that would be heated and blown into the shape of our bottles. We wanted a small bottle with a wide neck so our customers could easily pour formula powder into it. Small, single-serve bottles don't typically feature a wide neck, but Scott was such a dedicated partner, he wouldn't rest until he found an existing preform that would work for us, saving us hundreds of thousands of dollars we didn't have to spend to create a unique one. He also found an injection-molding company to blow the bottles, the label manufacturer—and even tracked down the seals to use for the caps.

I Am the Bottle

After a few months of driving up to Tennessee and all over Georgia to conduct our research and development, we were ready to pull the proverbial trigger and put the steps in place to eventually make a Nourish bottle. This was a big leap that would mean coming up with five figures to make the molds that would shape the preforms into our exclusive bottles. We thought we had all the details ironed out, but what if we had missed something? We didn't know what we didn't know. Before we even started thinking about how we would pay for it, we invited all the vendors we had met, representing our entire supply chain (mold manufacturer, label manufacturer, filler and co-packer, label printer), to Inmark for a daylong meeting. In the morning, we asked them to physically walk us through each step of the production process, with Lara standing in as "the bottle" and Stacey meticulously recording the intricacies of each step on a whiteboard. When we took a break, we noticed the men (all our suppliers were men) chuckling about something. We asked what was funny, and they said that in each of their twenty-plus years in the business they had never been in a meeting like that with one another, with every role represented and every step in the chain examined from each angle with all the players in the room. Nor had they ever been in a meeting in which the word *nipple* was used so often.

The experience proved invaluable to us. Because we sat in a room together, we discovered many things about the bottle design that needed to be changed before the molds were made, or we would incur huge costs. We saved a great deal of time and money by bringing together vendors who were seemingly unrelated to each other to let them each see the whole process and identify areas for improvement. As always, we took a systemic view, and we wanted each player to help us examine it. We were comfortable being the least knowledgeable people in the room because our lack of knowledge enabled us to notice things that experts would overlook.

Together, we noticed that the capping equipment would push down on the top of the cap and turn it to screw it on. But our cap wasn't the typical threaded water-bottle cap; it was shaped like a protective dome over the silicon nipple and sippy top. We observed that oval bottles will rotate differently going down an assembly line than round bottles, and that the sorter that would automatically feed bottles into case packs would not work easily with them.

And each of our partners detected potential issues in parts of the supply chain that were not their own. John Burleson, the filler, saw that the ridge under the threading was missing. To the rest of us it seemed unnecessary. But John knew that his equipment used that ridge to stabilize the bottles as they went down the line. Scott noted that our short bottles would use a preform intended for much larger bottles, so our plastic would be a bit heavier and add stability to the base of the bottle.

As the bottle took shape, we also had to consider our branding and storytelling. We took our notebooks and strolled the baby aisles in Target, Walmart, and supermarkets and scoped out what was there, Lara leading the way on product development, Stacey focusing on how we would tell our story. What we discovered from the shelves stocked with baby products is that those brands seemed very medicinal—think Similac and Enfamil. None of those names felt particularly warm and endearing, or like something you would want to snuggle up with at night. But we reasoned that if you are a new mother with a newborn baby, you're extremely cautious. You don't know anything and need to trust the brand. All the baby brands are positioned to be medically trustworthy.

Then we looked at the toddler products and noted all the primary colors and cartoon characters, like Tigger, Winnie the Pooh, and Elmo. We realized that if we were going to enter the toddler market, we didn't have enough money to compete with the big brands. How would we stand out? What were we going to do to be different? We came back to the idea that our water for babies and small children should be about health. It was about high trustworthiness and the purest water possible. We knew the packaging had to be clear to show pure water. Otherwise, how would you know what was in there?

Our friends had already become an indispensable resource, so we invited a bunch of our girlfriends to Lara's living room to brainstorm. We read them our long list of words and synonyms and explained that we wanted a brand name with very curvy letters because we wanted it to feel soft and inviting. Stacey put the word *nourish* on the list, and when we got to it, our friends agreed it sounded right. *Nourish* seemed to embody everything we wanted the water to be. It worked. Nourish was officially born.

We ultimately decided lime green looked fresh, happy, and healthy. The sippy caps and nipple tops would be green and so would the text on the clear bottles. Our baby water had the distinction of being new and unusual, yet absolutely part of how new moms would think about their earliest moments with their babies. We focused on language to evoke that sense of care, and Damon developed our signature image: one that looked like a heart and a water drop as well as a mother holding a baby. Stacey shopped language for the label to our team, and we picked our word palette— ways to be different yet familiar, to break new ground without scaring our customers at a time when life felt infinitely vulnerable.

Now we had a name, a product design, and a brand identity. We decided the marketing materials would feature black-and-white images of happy babies and kids. We recruited a local photographer to take pictures of Lara's neighbors' kids and Connor.

Grow Your Own Network

Yes, it was lucky that Lara's husband, Casey, worked for a beverage giant and that Stacey knew a graphic designer, that we had friends who helped start the company with us, and more friends and family who wanted to support us. But lots of people who also helped weren't in our immediate circles or directly connected to us. It is easy to get discouraged when you don't feel like you have the "right" or "important" contacts. But no matter who you are and where you come from, we *all* have networks. We have relatives, neighbors, people next to us in line at Panera, even people who sit next to us on a bus or an airplane. We tend to judge those around us based on their titles or where we meet them, without being curious enough to realize they can help, too. You never know where a chance conversation can lead you. Just being curious about people and generous about the value of their experiences can lead to meaningful relationships. We did not have an existing network with knowledge of the water-bottling industry at first. We built one in real time.

We also weren't plugged into a vibrant startup scene teeming with resources aimed at businesses like ours, so we had to be resourceful. That's the case for many entrepreneurs in legacy trades like manufacturing, logistics, retail, and professional services. Silicon Valley–inspired networks of well-funded research universities, accelerators, incubators, and venture capital firms nurture high-growth tech enterprises with lots of coaching and capital, whereas entrepreneurs in analog fields don't receive as much support.

"It's a two-tiered system," observes Drexel University economist Bruce Katz. "There's just no infrastructure of any heft."

You are not alone if it feels like you're navigating a "catch-as-catch-can" patchwork of nonprofits, community colleges, and outdated Small Business Development Centers (SBDCs) run by the Small Business Administration (SBA) to track down mentors and practical information about starting and operating a business. These educational resources are often disconnected from sources of funding too.

The economic ravages of COVID-19 exposed this disparity for

small businesses, especially disadvantaged firms, but also points to opportunities for reform. In Philadelphia, for example, Black-, brown-, and women-owned businesses overwhelmingly got shut out of the first two packages of PPP loans because they did not finance their businesses through major banks. But when an intermediary jumped in and connected business owners to community banks, credit unions, and financial technology firms to help business owners apply for the aid, their efforts paid off immediately. The Enterprise Center, an economic development nonprofit, quickly matched accountants with business owners to help them organize their books and offered free use of computers and the internet to those who didn't have access to online filing. The mobilization led to processing more than twenty thousand applications, according to the center's president, Della Clark. With these efforts, Pennsylvania improved from thirteenth in the nation in receiving PPP to eighth and enabled millions of dollars to flow to small firms on the brink of shutting down.

While entrepreneurial ecosystems may not always support small-business owners as much as they should, you can't let that discourage you. You have to look for ways to create your own network. It may take more time to find the right connections, but when you invest your energy in it, you can create your own safety net. It may feel daunting to pick up the phone or send a cold email, but you can't let that hold you back. You have to be creative and open-minded when asking for help, especially from other small-business owners. Ironically, some of the contacts to whom we didn't have a direct link—especially future suppliers, who, in addition to being kind, had a business incentive to help—ended up being our biggest champions. We approached them in pursuit of knowledge. We didn't have all the answers and we weren't afraid to admit what we didn't know. And as they shared their insights and experiences with us, they became invested in our success.

Nourish HQ

When we formally started Nourish Corporation in 2007, we relied on Lara's unflappable ability to strike up a conversation with anyone and on Stacey's legal training to keep us protected. We looked to family and friends and friends of friends for candid advice and help. The work was tough but gratifying. We had met some incredible people, and they graciously jumped on board. We didn't leave our day jobs at Insomnia just yet. We still needed the safety net of our consulting work to pay the bills.

We were no-frills in everything we did. One afternoon, after one of our meetings at Inmark, Scott Curlee's packaging company, he and an associate noticed the two of us deep in conversation in our car in the parking lot. Since we usually met in coffee shops, our kitchens, or as we drove to meetings, our cars often doubled as conference rooms. Scott teased us that we were loitering. The next time we went back to Inmark, we brought a sign with us that read NOURISH BOARD ROOM and hung it in front of a parking space. That became the first Nourish HQ, and it felt great.

After months of road trips and research, we had suppliers lined up waiting for the green light. We had our branding. We had market research. Since the bottle prototypes would not be manufactured until we landed our first order and figured out how to fund it, we fashioned our own model out of duct tape and stayed up late typing up the first labels to adhere to it to make it look official. This was in the days before 3D printing, so duct tape had to do.

Now we needed customers.

LEVEL-UP LESSONS:
CHAPTER 3

- You don't have to be an expert to solve a problem. A lack of knowledge can be a blessing. Most innovation comes from what you notice, not from what you know. Give yourself permission to have a big idea in an area that is not in your area of expertise.

- Get comfortable with ambiguity. Not having all the answers at the outset can lead you to new ideas and solutions you never would have considered.

- Share your ideas with others. They are too busy to steal your idea. If you don't share it, no one can help.

- Your network = your net worth. A network is a living, growing organism. You can start building one anywhere. To grow a network, you need to feed it.

- Look at your larger ecosystem—your customers, suppliers, partners, competitors. All can be sources of capital and value.

4

⋮

CUSTOMERS + COMMERCE = CAPITAL

t wasn't long before we took our rudimentary Nourish model on the road to find distributors and retailers to sell our bottled water. One day, we raced down to a modest corporate building near the Atlanta airport to meet with a family-run business called the Paradies Shops. Now it's a North American chain, but back then, the locally owned company operated newsstands and gift shops in a handful of airports. A friend of Lara's, Janace Harding, whom she had met through a women's real estate industry networking group, was working with Paradies and offered to introduce Nourish as a potential new product. Janace had called us that morning and told us that if we could get to Paradies in an hour we could speak at their meeting. We jumped in the car and prepped along the way.

Despite not having a polished deck or dazzling prototype, we were determined to take our shot.

Armed with our sales pitch and audacity, we presented to the friendly buyer and a few of her team members sitting around a modest conference table. Images of our concept, our logo, and our duct-tape model got passed around the room. Lara regaled them with our origin story and financials, and Stacey talked through our brand proposition and marketing plan. Together, and definitely on the fly, we refined our case for taking up precious real estate on their limited shelf space. In airports across the country, their customers would be ducking into Paradies shops to replace the baby bottle left on the kitchen counter in the mad rush to the airport. Or a harried mom with a squirming toddler would want a quick solution to thirst and a fun distraction. Nourish was the answer they didn't know they needed. The conversation shifted from proof of concept to price points, and we knew we had something. Still, we capped our expectations, knowing that a good meeting did not automatically become a contract.

Start Small. Think Big. Scale Fast.

Buoyed by our mom brain trust and the responses from our suppliers, we originally set our sights on selling to big grocery chains. A friend of Lara's worked as a facility project manager for one of the largest, and she agreed to introduce us to a local buyer who could explain the process of getting new products in the stores. In our conversations, he shared that shelf space was a prized commodity and told us what it would take to get on the shelves and stay. The buyer loved the Nourish concept and thought it would sell. The prospect he represented—becoming an overnight sensation by getting our startup shelf space at a national retailer—tempted us, but we stopped ourselves before we went down that road. We admitted to ourselves that we weren't ready; we hadn't even manufactured the actual bottles yet.

While we could go to boutiques and place a handful of bottles for sale, a small test for a grocer the size he repped required us to supply fifty-plus stores. The scale of opportunity had to be met by the competence of our business model. As our advisers confirmed, we would only get one chance to impress the major players, so there would be little or no margin for error. Inventory and marketing had to be optimal and successful across multiple locations. If our bottles just sat on shelves and didn't sell through because we didn't have the marketing dollars to make a splash, we would fail before we even got started.

Retailers like Kroger, Walmart, and Target would want to price the product comparably to other bottled-water products and children's beverages like juice boxes, but that would squeeze our profit margins. Our cost to make the product would remain high until we achieved economies of scale by manufacturing larger orders down the road. We decided to start small; with boutique stores we could learn the ropes, have some price flexibility, and make mistakes. Our mantra became "Start small. Think big. Scale fast."

We had to think counterintuitively about how to reach customers. We kept going back to something Sara Blakely shared with us when we first asked her for advice. She told us that when she launched Spanx, the obvious place to sell her footless pantyhose would have been the hosiery section. But if she had started there, she would never have had the money to compete with the big brands that dominated that space, like Donna Karan and L'eggs. Spanx wouldn't have stood out. And so, she thought to herself, "Where else can I be where the need for my product is the highest and where people are a little less comparison sensitive, and I can solve their problem right away and learn from them?" She went to the formal dress section and talked her way into setting up a little display on the counter, where Spanx could become an impulse buy because, of course, you always buy the dress first.

We had to figure out our corollary to Sara's fancy dress department.

Nourish was a spill-proof bottle of water that you could either use to mix formula for a baby or hand to a thirsty toddler. Where do you need that the most? Probably not in your house, right? In the comfort of home, you have a full kitchen and lots of options. But when you're out and about, you don't always have a solution ready at hand. The allure of a big retailer as our first major client had to be weighed against our readiness to launch and our ability to reach customers at their greatest point of need. *Where would the appeal of Nourish be high and the competitive choices few?*

Lara could speak from experience. She was still scarred from the time she and Casey flew from Atlanta with baby Connor to visit Casey's grandparents on the Upper Peninsula of Michigan. Of course, they missed the connection, and feeding time coincided with their layover. Stranded at the airport with a screaming infant, Lara and Casey could not find room temperature water in any of the terminal stores to fix Connor's bottle. The memory provided the perfect use case. Nourish was tailor-made for airports. Air travelers cannot be price sensitive, in addition to being a captive audience. With luggage already checked through security, customers are primed to pay a premium for a ready solution. As we tallied up initial startup costs and decent profit margins, we realized the airport provided a unique chance to test market and costs. Paradies was smaller game than a major grocery chain, but they offered us the smarter value: available customers, low competition, and a premium marketplace.

We waited on pins and needles to hear back from Paradies. Soon after our pitch, Lara received an email from the buyer and immediately dialed Stacey in her State House office to tell her Paradies planned to feature Nourish. We had landed our first customer! But our customer had become a reality before our inventory. In launching a company that relied on a physical product rather than our personal intellectual capital, we had to adjust our mindsets to the challenge of managing a supply chain. Both of us had become used to selling fast because we knew we could simply increase our own productivity to scale. Leveling up a manufacturing business required a different approach, and the timing didn't always align with need. Often, small-business owners have to take advantage of opportunity when it arrives—not when they are ready. We knew we had to start small: Paradies versus big box. We had been ready to think big: pitching to a client before we had a product. Now we had to scale fast: deliver Nourish to Paradies or risk losing a golden moment.

Even though we had refined the design and lined up the suppliers, the water bottles still needed to be manufactured. By taking

Paradies's order, we would commit to delivering three cases of bottles to each of their stores. Now we needed to go back to our suppliers and ask what the minimum order they could make for us was. Just to fill the Paradies order, we found out we would be looking at fifty-thousand bottles and twenty-five thousand nipples and sippy tops with caps. The product run would need to be far larger than what we would initially sell to Paradies, but we had to say yes. Although we had begun to raise startup capital, we now had to finalize how we were going to pay for the molds for the nipples, the sippy tops, the collars, and the bottles, as well as the raw materials for the bottles, seals, and labels. We also had to factor in the cost of manual assembly. Because of the unique bottle shape, English Mountain Springs would have to seal them by hand. All told, we estimated we would need close to three hundred thousand dollars for the molds and another hundred thousand dollars to fill the order.

Often small businesses have enough cash for the known costs, and they can be hesitant to strike out for more without a clear sight line on unexpected expenses and how to cover them. Sometimes, scaling fast depends on our earlier admonition: Get comfortable with ambiguity. Accepting the Paradies order was one of those times when our ability to embrace uncertainty made all the difference. We had to believe we would figure it out given our prep work and the quality of our idea. We just had to start working our network and have faith in the process of being curious and asking questions.

Stacey was exceptionally comfortable about letting things play out because this was how she approached her fiction writing. Lara discovered this early in our working relationship. One day while we were going over a consulting project at Lara's dining-room table,

Lara noticed a quizzical look on Stacey's face and asked what she was thinking about. She seemed far away for a moment. Stacey smiled sheepishly and revealed that one of the characters in the romantic suspense novel she was writing was stuck in her mind. Stacey, who wrote books under the pen name Selena Montgomery, was befuddled. She couldn't figure out how to resolve a dilemma in which the character had not operated as she'd expected. Lara was taken aback. She assumed that Stacey, who usually seemed to carefully consider all the angles before she made a move, had meticulously mapped out each step of her characters *before* she started writing. But that was not the case at all. Stacey explained that while she did carefully outline and detail each part of a story, the protagonists and supporting cast often diverged from what she'd initially plotted and took actions that veered far from what she expected. Lara joked about whether she should worry about the voices in Stacey's head. Stacey laughed—she'd gotten used to knowing what the end goal should be but didn't always anticipate how each scene would play out. It turned out that this approach—questioning, pausing, letting different possible answers simmer for a bit instead of rushing to make quick decisions—helped us persevere as business partners in the face of the unknown.

Second-Class Startup

Though we had gotten ourselves to a product through bootstrapping, the shift from idea to scaled production cost more than we could personally finance. Neither of us worried, though, because we had an actual purchase order from a real customer. With Paradies in hand and other clients seeming likely to purchase, we mapped out how much it would cost to grow our company as orders came in. We accounted for manufacturing, marketing, shipping, and staffing. Revenue would start to flow eventually, but we wanted to have sufficient capital to make the smartest choices we could for what came next. We assumed potential investors would jump at the chance to grab an early stake in our company. But that's not the way it worked.

We decided to raise $1.5 million to fund the initial product run and marketing for the next year. With our innovative product, our high-profile advisers, and stellar résumés, we never expected that our company would be treated like a second-class startup. Yet that was how it felt when we started talking to angel investors and venture capitalists. Investors thought it was creative and unique, and anybody who had kids immediately understood the problem. Of course, starting it in the same city as Coca-Cola's headquarters seemed like a great way to set the stage for the beverage giant to acquire it. But in the end, their underwhelmed response was, "Meh. It's a bottled-water company."

We had run into unicorn syndrome. Atlanta's entrepreneurial ecosystem, like many others around the country at the time, was hyperfocused on tech and startups with a lightning-speed growth trajectory that could potentially grow into the billion dollar companies known in Silicon Valley as unicorns. To our dismay, we quickly discovered that investors were looking for dazzling technology, three-year exits, and gigantic returns of ten to twenty times their investment. A bottled-water company is not going to go public or be acquired for tens of millions of dollars in three years. The business, like much of the manufacturing side, is too asset-intense. In 2007, the investment community was more interested in companies without physical inventory or heavy equipment and in solutions that could be solved with an app. Think Facebook or Mint. Instead, Nourish looked like the workhorse small businesses that pull the economy—and were considered just as unattractive for sexy capital.

In the world of capital for startups, the options are slim: self-funding, friends and family investment, loans, credit, or outside investors. The seed round wasn't going to work out like we hoped, and we had put in what we could. This mainly left borrowing from lenders or getting credit from our suppliers.

When we updated Scott Curlee at Inmark, he provided credit. Impressed by our progress and our customers, he offered to pay for some of the molds and amortize costs over time. Essentially, he would charge us a little more for each bottle until we had paid for the molds that he fronted the costs to buy for us. On the borrowing front, we didn't want to try to apply for a small-business loan from a bank just yet. For one, we didn't have the cash flow the bank would want to see to guarantee we could pay back the loan. This meant the bank would want to use our personal assets as collateral. Neither of us could afford to sign personal guarantees or put up our homes as collateral. We both had major personal financial obligations to aging parents and new infants that took precedence. Moreover, we were both still paying off college and graduate school loans.

Another prong to the decision wasn't just where to get the money but when. The timing of money matters as much as the amount and whom it comes from. We knew that one day, if the orders were large enough, we would need to take out financing to buy equipment and tooling to automate our production instead of relying on manual assembly. Without an investor at that point, we would be on our own. And if we already had debt on our balance sheet, getting a loan would be more difficult and more expensive. Borrowing would have to wait.

Your Network Is Your Net Worth

So we turned to our most likely capital market: friends. We had not come this far to turn down the deal with Paradies. Knowing that we had built a solid sales model and had a product ready to go, we turned to raising money close to home. We had lunch with a couple of friends who understood our ambition. Sharing our updates, we explained our status: that we had all the pricing on the molds and that we'd landed our first retail customer. Even if we weren't ready for the opportunity, the news buoyed their excitement and ours.

After hearing all this, one of our friends asked how much we really needed to do it. We told her we were still talking to investors. But she replied that she believed in us and genuinely wanted to help. The others at the table offered to invest too and promised to ask their friends. We had both raised money before, but the small capital infusion that helped us launch suddenly turned into a true friends and angels round of investment.

At the start, the friends and family round of money came largely from Lara's contacts, which revealed another hurdle for small start-ups. Though we had both come from modest beginnings, Lara's previous work had taken her into real estate and finance, two industries where investing five thousand dollars or twenty-five thousand dollars in a concept made sense. But it also helped that Lara had an extensive résumé on the commercial side. Stacey had proven herself to be a prolific political fundraiser, having outraised both of her 2006 opponents combined and raising more money than almost any candidate running for the state legislature that cycle. However, because her network was mostly in nonprofit or government spaces, she found it difficult to convert those relationships into business investment. For many small or microbusinesses, not having any such relationships presents an unscalable obstacle.

That said, you don't know the strength of your network until you ask. Part of our growth came from Lara's willingness to share our story. Stacey learned not to assume that those who gave political dollars would recoil at the thought of investing in a commercial venture. Each time she added names to the cap table, Lara's effectiveness inspired her to make another ask. The networks we had rarely overlapped; but together, they formed a financial safety net that let us take the leap of faith to order our first run. And then another. And another.

As we continued adding boutiques and other customers, we were able to show progress and add more investors to the pool. Lara kept our investors up to speed on our status, particularly when the news wasn't promising. Comfort with ambiguity is a plus as a business owner, as we've seen, but you should never expect that from your investors. By keeping them apprised and by carefully tending their funds, we cultivated a strong investor group that stuck with us. This meant that our network continued to grow and showed resilience to setbacks. Even Stacey got better at securing funds to grow our company. Ultimately, we raised $231,000 to get the bottles made, plus some extra for marketing. Our friends who contributed to Nourish's launch and growth were not billionaire investors, though of course they (and we) were fortunate that they had the means to bet ten or fifteen thousand dollars on us. They were willing to take a chance because we asked and then we told.

Three Cs of Growth

It would be our friends and our relentless pursuit of customers that helped us not only fill the Paradies order but start generating real cash flow to scale our company. Once we could make bottles for stores to sell to actual customers—moms or dads in the airport— that commerce gave the company the capital it needed to grow. The formula is what we call the Three Cs of Growth: customers + commerce = capital. Customers add value no matter what. They provide the *revenue* so that you can fund some portion of your business. Even if they don't give you a profit on day one, they add value to your business in every way. They offer feedback to improve your product. They make your company worth more because people pay you. Without customers and the *commerce* from selling to them, what you have is a hobby.

The majority of dollars that enter a small business comes in the form of revenue from customers and commerce. Yet policy makers have long operated as though banks were the natural supply chain of capital to small businesses. The Great Recession of 2008 and the COVID-19 pandemic exposed the truth. In 2020, Congress sent billions in pandemic aid down the supply chain to bolster small businesses rocked by quarantine and shortages. But most of the money did not make its way to small businesses. Instead, it flowed to banks' real clients: mid-market and larger companies. What became clear is that the true supply chain of capital to small businesses is commerce, and when that is interrupted, small businesses flounder.

Jonathan Ford put himself through Southern Polytechnic College in Marietta, Georgia, by working on construction sites around town. But he dreamed of owning his own construction firm and eventually started talking up his plans with tradespeople he met on jobs in Atlanta, including at Hartsfield-Jackson Atlanta International Airport. He first went out on his own in 2012 as a consultant. He always believed he would have to self-fund his business if he wanted to grow it. Black business owners start companies with less capital than white counterparts and are much less likely to secure bank loans because they have less family wealth. As a Black entrepreneur without many assets, Jonathan didn't think he would find a lender.

Jonathan didn't have much savings. He also didn't think investors would be interested in backing a young construction firm. But what he did have was a relentless drive to talk to as many people as he could to get the word out about his services and then to develop a reputation for exceptional work and attention to detail. He knew his success hinged on building lasting relationships with clients. Many business owners focus on getting the first customer order or contract, but really, you should focus on the tenth order or contract. Because to get the tenth order you have to deliver, and that's what makes a business sustainable over time. Jonathan focused on sales *and* outstanding quality.

"When you don't have funding and things like that, it's all about word of mouth and letting people know your needs and desires and leveraging the relationships that you've created over the years," he told us, looking back on the early days of building the Jon Smith Group, now a multimillion-dollar contracting firm.

Because he established trust with his customers from the start, he eventually was able to finesse how quickly he got paid. Some clients agreed to what's called an "early payment discount." It meant that the client would pay him sooner than the due date out of their own pockets *at a discount* and *before* they were paid by their own clients. He made a little less, but at the same time these strategic arrangements enabled Jonathan to grow because he unlocked cash flow instead of waiting thirty, sixty, or one hundred twenty days for accounts to be settled. (Note: This tactic can work with small customers but beware of trying it on large customers. Because large customers know they have the power in the relationship, they will often take the discount and still pay late because they know they can get away with it.) With revenue flowing into the business, Jonathan could afford to take on more clients and hire his first employee. It was a scary prospect to have someone relying on him for a paycheck. But he decided he had to do it to grow. In a sweet twist of fate, his very first hire would be a general superintendent to oversee upgrades and renovations to doors, conveyor systems, and ceilings inside Concourse E at the airport where Jonathan once worked when he was starting out. Now he returned to the site as a business owner.

In 2018, the NFL arrived in Atlanta to interview local business owners to work on Super Bowl LIII. Jonathan's firm was much smaller than many of the contractors bidding on the construction jobs. Still, he figured he had nothing to lose. He and his general superintendent, Alsee Rutledge, made an impassioned fifteen-minute sales pitch at the Georgia World Congress Center for an opportunity that would change the fate of his firm.

"We told them about what we'd done, how creative we've been in all the hours spent to make projects happen, and how we were outside-of-the-box thinkers. And I think they just felt the passion that we had for it," he recalls.

A few weeks later, in a top-secret phone call from the NFL, Jonathan was surprised to find out his company won the contract to build the media infrastructure for the big game. They would install the wiring, the trailers, the mobile offices, and anything CBS would need for the production of the broadcast. Jonathan scrambled to interview and onboard 145 plumbers, electricians, and carpenters for the massive undertaking, which had to be completed within six weeks. When it was all said and done, the NFL named the Jon Smith Group "Minority Supplier of the Year." The recognition cemented the company's stellar reputation and led to bigger, more lucrative contracts. Today, the Jon Smith Group employs fifteen and generates between $3 million and $5 million in annual revenues from its broad portfolio of commercial and specialized construction work and products.

Selling, Selling, Selling

Just the way Jonathan homed in on relationships with customers, once we landed Paradies, our path to revenue, to growth, and to scale was to keep selling and seeking out new accounts. Now our company owned tens of thousands of unsold Nourish bottles. Towers of cardboard boxes occupying a corner of the spare room in Lara's home that doubled as a playroom for Connor never let us forget the clock was ticking. We rolled up our sleeves and devoted as much time as we could to spreading the word about our water bottles to just about anyone who would listen.

Lara had long admired a dreamy children's boutique in Buckhead called baby braithwaite. The trendsetting, upscale shop featured adorable gifts, baby registry staples, and nursery furniture set against an angelic all-white décor below a glittering chandelier. We didn't know the owner, but that didn't stop Lara from strolling in one day with some of our bottles and asking to meet with the founder, Chaffee Braithwaite. Chaffee wasn't there that day. But Lara kept going back and asking to meet with her. When they finally talked, Lara inquired if we could set up a table in the store one Saturday afternoon to chat with customers about Nourish in hopes we might be able to sell the bottles to her high-end clientele. Chaffee agreed, and we arranged a date. She would become a fan and even introduced us to a local photographer named Alice Park, whose gorgeous images of children adorned the walls of the shop. She ended up taking cute pictures of Connor and his friends frolicking with a hose in Lara's grassy backyard for the new marketing brochures Stacey had designed.

With news that we could set up at baby braithwaite, we raced to Costco to purchase a folding table and chairs, a white tablecloth, and shiny green apple–colored ribbon. Next stop was HomeGoods for glass carafes to fill with eye-catching lime jellybeans and green rock candy. We bought picture frames for our little flyers since we didn't have fancy backdrops for our display. We pulled on our cute Nourish tees, put on our smiles, and talked up our story and the bottles once again. This would become our regular routine as we drove all over Atlanta to any fun run or church picnic or health fair that would have us. We got really good at setting up tables quickly, taking them back down, and packing and lugging boxes ourselves. We looked for PR any way we could get it. We pitched Nourish to mom bloggers and local radio stations, and during one local TV appearance we even got the anchors and the production crew to try our bottles. To our delight, they discovered the spill-proof sippy top lids were a great solution to preventing spills on the set.

The bottles sold well at Paradies, and their team became personally committed to our business. They were excited that they were the first ones to carry this product. And they gave us feedback on packaging and pricing. Like our other partners, they didn't mind that we didn't know all the answers to everything. In fact, they thought it was exciting that they got to be a part of something that was just taking off.

The next step was to get the word out beyond Atlanta and find customers in new markets. To do that, we set off for the Las Vegas Convention Center and the mother of all trade shows for the children's industry, All Baby and Child, known as the ABC Show. If you're a giant like Carter's, you spend millions of dollars to set up fancy displays at trade shows, with massive teams to build and break down. But for Nourish, it was just the two of us and Lara's mom, Beverly O'Connor, who graciously joined us to help.

The three of us flew out a day early and had everything shipped to our hotel room. We couldn't afford to hire local union workers to help us set up our space. So each morning of the trade show we rose early and made multiple trips on foot, carrying boxes from our Vegas hotel along what felt like miles of city blocks to the exhibition hall. Lara's mom, ever the trouper, joked that she thought we were trying to kill her with all the walking in 110-degree heat.

The trip seemed to be well worth the literal sweat equity we all put in that week. In addition to returning home with thirty to forty orders ranging from a few cases for boutiques to a few dozen cases for larger stores, we got an education on deal terms and credit. We had no idea that buyers for retailers would ask us directly how much credit we'd extend them on an order. Because Paradies and baby braithwaite had been close contacts, this was our first encounter with the dreaded *net 30* or longer. On that trip and in the days after, we learned about the seemingly normal expectation that there would be a delay in payment for our products. Some larger buyers would ask us to give them two thousand dollars' worth of bottles that they could pay for in thirty days, or dangle the possibility of purchasing five thousand dollars' worth—and then how many days would we give them to pay? We had no way to assess if this was a good deal for us, or even whether these retailers could be counted on for the payments they promised. Small businesses don't have a real window into the balance sheets of other private companies. Like many of our counterparts at the trade show, we relied on the name recognition of a particular store and our guts in lieu of real data. For example, we heard that The Pump Station & Nurtury in Santa Monica was a magnet for celebrity parents; shops like that were high on our list, even if we might not like the terms.

Some retail buyers paid us with a purchasing card, which let us write down the credit card number and run the card when we shipped. That was utopia. But a lot of buyers—in fact, most—wouldn't do that. The larger or more seasoned retailers understood the cost of capital with a small startup: zero. To a one, they told us we had to offer terms or forgo the deal—either take the order at our expense or pass up the chance at real revenue. Of course, we chose the orders. When we flew home to Atlanta, we were exhausted but exhilarated, with lots of new customers for Nourish. We rushed back to our makeshift office to start packing boxes. But we had no clue who was going to pay when.

We had been packing the cases ourselves in Lara's house and driving to FedEx or UPS to ship them. When we ran low, we would drive Lara's Explorer up to Tennessee to English Mountain Springs and load up the trunk with as many boxes as we could to replenish our stock. But as our customer base grew, so did our need for physical expansion. We needed more space, and that's when we lucked into meeting Kevin Willis, a seven-foot former power forward for the Atlanta Hawks, who was in the process of launching a private fashion label for tall men.

In a previous position, Lara had worked for Shaquille O'Neal's sneaker brand and mutual contacts connected Kevin to Lara for some advice. Over lunch one afternoon, Lara told him about Nourish. Kevin asked where our office was. Lara laughed and admitted the truth: we still met in our cars or in one of our homes. For high profile meetings, we used the startup trick of lunch or dinner meetings in nice but reasonably priced restaurants. No overhead and an attentive waitstaff. An entrepreneur himself, Kevin offered up a suite above the private atelier he used for his fashion line. The building turned out to be a short drive from Lara's home. It would become our first real Nourish HQ, and not a moment too soon.

As soon as we set up a formal place to work and a new spot for our inventory and shipping, business picked up tremendously. Our supply chain was within driving distance, which let us keep an eye on quality control and scramble to adjust when things went awry. Once, we got a call from a customer that the collar was leaking (not good for spill-proof bottled water). The head engineer at our molding company drove forty-five minutes to Atlanta, and together we cut open a few collars to diagnose what was wrong with the threading. The next week, we all got in the car and drove four hours to Tennessee to see if the fix we had developed would work. One of our smartest choices had been to keep our partners close in the early days of our company. While others advised us to go to China for cheaper parts, we had to weigh the inexpensive cost of materials against the risk of delays or quality control with overseas suppliers and potential liability exposure. We evaluated how we could best leverage our precious dollars while also guaranteeing the quality of our product. In the end, we stuck with local suppliers and learned that being able to work together and quickly fix issues in those crucial first months was way more important than shaving costs in the short run.

Nourish in Demand

By the summer of 2008, we had more orders coming in by the day from retailers all over the country. Each work day ended with one of us stopping by the UPS Store or FedEx to drop off cases of product. Stacey focused on tracking down the new customers who sometimes didn't pay us on time, even with the generous terms retailers set for themselves. Nourish continued to retain repeat customers in Atlanta, who we needed to keep happy. We set up a website, and suddenly, we had direct-to-consumer orders to ship. All the while, we were still trying to unwind Insomnia Consulting so we could devote ourselves to Nourish. We were multitasking frenetically, but with competing obligations and a company growth spurt, key items fell through the cracks. As consultants, we could cover every aspect of a job between the two of us. Research, writing, and presentations simply required more time and effort. Running a manufacturing business needed bodies: contractors to label bottles or to pack and ship boxes of product. Friends and family volunteered to help us, and we added an enterprising Georgia Tech intern interested in learning about sales and marketing. We patched together a short-term solution to our labor needs, yet success required full-time assistance. But as small-business owners learn as they expand, finding the right help turned out to be much more challenging than expected.

LEVEL-UP LESSONS: CHAPTER 4

- Your biggest dream customer is *not* your best first customer. Start small while thinking big.

- Focus on the Three Cs of Growth: customers, commerce, and capital. If these three start flowing, then you shift into gear and begin turning a flywheel of growth.

- Look beyond the first order. Many businesses are one and done. Your goal is to get the tenth order. Be sure you can deliver the first order well or you won't see the tenth order.

- There are no second-class startups. Just because an investor or a lender says no does not mean your business is bad. You have to find the right source of capital for you, at the right time, and for the right use.

5

⋮

HIRE PATIENCE.
HIRE PATIENTLY.

When we first started Nourish, we didn't have to look too far to find people to pitch in. All sorts of friends, neighbors, relatives, and yes, strangers who became helpful friends got swept up in our tornado of momentum. As they shared their encouragement, talents, and network with us, gratefully included them in our storm. We welcomed their advice and enthusiastic support. But there came a point, amid the frenzy to get Nourish off the ground, when we realized that even free assistance came at a cost. Like many new business owners, we faced a mismatch between people's enthusiasm for launching a startup and their willingness to wait for a potential payout. Over time, whether with partners or employees, we faced difficult decisions on how to find team members who could cope with the long hours, setbacks, and delayed-gratification mindset it would take to scale a business to profit.

Free Help Has a Price

When a company is starting out, the most effective partners are those who share your passion and understand your limited finances. Often, these helpmates are friends who see the allure of opportunity, ones who bring special skill sets that can add to the likelihood of success. High-quality talent at rock-bottom prices can be a seductive option, especially when years of camaraderie seem to merge seamlessly into a common vision for success. But for most small businesses, the array of talent available comes with strings attached. The perfect person tends to already be on someone else's payroll or pursuing dreams of their own.

When we met for lunch on the day Lara conceived of baby water, we were already a team. We were running Insomnia Consulting together, but Stacey's major focus was her campaign for the state legislature. She'd asked two fellow Spelman College alumnae to join her quest. Monika Majors was a rising marketing star at a Fortune 500 company, and she'd come on board as Stacey's campaign manager despite having no previous political experience. They'd reasoned that an effective campaign for office, like a good product launch, lies in the ability to communicate a vision and reach constituents. Financing a campaign required money, and Che Watkins brought years of experience as a high-powered banker. Together with a third friend, Camille Johnson, the campaign team was on track to outraise their opponents and defeat two better-known, better-connected candidates. Stacey's campaign would end after the July primary, but the team she assembled had promise that stretched beyond politics.

When Nourish began to take shape, we looked at our skills like a jigsaw puzzle, and we realized Monika and Che were perfect additions. With their inclusion, our pieces came together. Product experience—check. Legal skills—check. Marketing—check. Finance—check. Together, the four of us—Lara, Stacey, Monika, and Che—were primed to tackle every obstacle. Except reality. Monika and Che had full-time, high-intensity jobs that demanded their first loyalty. The two of us, who held more ownership in the fledgling business, had greater flexibility because we worked for ourselves. The contrast became clearer and clearer as the company grew. Despite their capacity and their enthusiasm, Monika and Che just did not have the time.

By November 2008, as we were ramping up sales to Paradies, baby braithwaite, and other retailers, we realized we had to be honest about how Nourish could scale from a brainstorm in Lara's living room to a thriving business with orders to fill. More precisely, we had to confront the consequences of changing the business's ownership to meet this hard truth. Friendship—and shared imagination—can launch an idea but cannot always grow it. When other people's money comes into play and real obligations are made, you have to be honest about what is expected from every team member. We had thought about NDAs and stock certificates, but we forgot to lay out concrete obligations because no one was receiving a paycheck.

Often, business owners avoid tough discussions because they worry about the personal fallout. That is a valid and healthy concern. But what is worse is the erosion of relationships because we mistake cowardice for compassion. Tensions had already grown palpable, and we were working around one another, not with one another. When launching Insomnia Consulting, we had set ground rules, but we failed to have a similar conversation with Monika and Che. That was our fault, and it made a tough situation infinitely more complicated. To meet the difficulties to come, have the hard talks up front and write your decisions down. Don't allow the promise of future success obscure the responsibility to fix current hardships. Even if you aren't paying each other in cash, there's a cost when things fall apart.

Co-ownership has a very specific set of complexities. Hiring employees also carries risks, especially when you are hiring from within your personal circle. One part of Nourish's appeal was that it came from a new mom, and that we focused on women as a core part of our dynamic. We raised money from women who often didn't get invited to early-stage opportunities. We sought advice from women who had made good. And we had already struck out on our own and demonstrated the flexibility of entrepreneurship. One of our first-round investors was looking for a transition into self-employment, and Nourish struck her as a golden chance to test her wings. We were careful to put together an employment agreement to keep the work and investor roles separate. But we were still a long way from being able to afford real salaries. When we were introduced to another woman who had an extensive marketing background, we signed an agreement that acknowledged the modest salary we could offer.

To introduce Nourish to more customers, we packaged pristine white boxes containing Nourish bottles and our glossy brochure, all tied up with lime green ribbon. Our new staff joined us in the unglamorous work of assembling and shipping these boxes, which were intended as gifts for celebrities and influencers who we hoped would adopt Nourish and share our story. With some hustle, we even snagged an invite to the 2009 Primetime Emmy Awards to showcase Nourish in suites brimming with swag for Hollywood royalty. We and our two new teammates flew to Los Angeles and enjoyed the fun of celebrity watching on the red carpet, shopping on Melrose, and treating ourselves to famous Sprinkles Cupcakes in Beverly Hills—in addition to the satisfaction of finally seeing our hard work grab high-profile attention.

But upon our return to Atlanta, reality set in.

As our COO, Stacey took on the role of HR and legal counsel. Part of her job was to draft employment agreements and, on the other side, to listen to employee concerns. The glamour of L.A. and glowing press reviews suggested that Nourish had arrived. Without steady cash beyond what we'd raised, our compensation agreements relied on revenue milestones, but we could not guarantee how long it would take to reach them. When employees can easily "see" the success of a company, explaining the transition from attention to profit is difficult. Our team could walk into the Atlanta airport and look at the bottles on the shelves. They knew parents who'd scooped up bottles at their favorite boutique. This sparked pointed questions about the business model, questions about the sales strategy, and ultimately, questions about leadership.

For staff used to regular paychecks, the vagaries of a startup's finances can be impossible to accept. We could afford the investment in a trip to Hollywood and risk funds on a strategy to boost recognition, but guaranteeing the recurring costs of salaries carries heavy implications. The team we hired had the sophistication to discuss these issues, but when perception and reality collided, perception won. While we had been clear about the fact that we needed steady revenue to agree to higher pay, they didn't understand how long that might take—or how we would measure its arrival.

One challenge of being an entrepreneur is being honest enough, both with yourself and with your partners, about how long building the business can take. Part of the enthusiasm of being a startup comes from believing that if you just put in your work, you're going to reach more customers, more sales, and eventually more revenue. But it's difficult to acknowledge that "getting there" takes much longer than you imagined. A three-year business plan is probably a six-year journey to profit. So it is critical to manage the expectations of anyone you bring onto your team and to clearly define roles and compensation right up front. You must make sure they grasp the long, winding road ahead. You must hire *patience* and give your team the information to understand the wait.

Help Wanted

It is a pivotal choice to start paying other people to work for you. Bringing on staff, whether a full-time hire or a contractor, whether you are paying in cash or with equity in the company, is a huge commitment. For small-business owners, the timing hinges on the predictability of customers and commerce. And let's face it, no one has a crystal ball. It's no surprise that Black and brown entrepreneurs, who have a harder time securing capital, also have a hard time hiring. In Philadelphia, for example, only twelve hundred of the thirty thousand small businesses owned by POC have employees. Becoming an employer can put an unusually heavy burden on the owner's income if their business isn't backed by private investor dollars and/or personal wealth and assets.

If you're feeling overwhelmed by the prospect of expanding your team, you are not the only one. Fewer entrepreneurs are becoming employers. In 2005, approximately one in five U.S. small businesses created one or more jobs. That number dipped to one in ten by 2018. Business owners unequivocally ranked finding talent as one of their biggest obstacles, John Dearie, founder and president of the Center for American Entrepreneurship (CAE), learned when he surveyed small-business owners in the aftermath of the Great Recession. The seismic shifts caused by the COVID-19 pandemic have only made it harder. Two thirds of small firms surveyed by SCORE (Service Corps of Retired Executives) in 2021 say that "hiring the right talent" is their biggest worry. Small businesses are at an even greater disadvantage because they don't have the capital to entice talent with competitive wages or expensive benefits and perks. Small businesses also don't typically have the human resources capacity to even recruit in such an aggressive environment. "It is incredibly lonely when it is just you or a small team. You don't have an HR manager or a compliance officer. You don't have a CFO. You are doing it all by yourself. And it is why startups are so fragile," Dearie explained.

One solution that didn't exist when we were building Nourish is the explosion of new online marketplaces that help small-business owners screen and hire freelance and part-time talent. This is an area of entrepreneurship that has really taken off since 2016, according to CAE. Our friend, serial entrepreneur Genevieve Bos, says she's seen firsthand how these new digital resources are "game changers for new businesses" that don't have the bandwidth or in-house resources to recruit staff.

From ex-McKinsey consultants to executive coaches to CMOs for hire, this new crop of startups is helping to place experts in temporary gigs, even handling the onboarding paperwork, payroll, health benefits, and compliance. We Are Rosie, for example, offers entrepreneurs turnkey access to more than nine thousand marketing freelancers from Fortune 100 C-suite executives to self-taught creatives. Clients can use the service as needed, depending on the ebb and flow of their business. Another new entrant is HireRunner. It's the brainchild of Arlan Hamilton, who also founded Backstage Capital, a venture firm that invests in underrepresented entrepreneurs. HireRunner matches small companies and solopreneurs with temporary executive assistants and other entry-level operations and HR staff.

Hire Patiently

For a new business owner, there is constant tension between the need for more help and the impulse to hire the first time you have a little bit of capital and more prospective customers. This is true whether you're bringing on a freelancer or full-time, salaried help. Not only do you have to hire patience, but *you also have to hire patiently*. In the early days, finding the "right" team member is more important than the "right now" team member. Mindset matters more than skill set for an employee of a rapidly evolving new business. As you grow, you will need to find people with more sophisticated or specific expertise. Keep in mind, for example, that a bookkeeper may be fine initially, but eventually you may need a CFO to handle more complex financials, and plan for that. At the same time, if you try to hire the person you will need three years too early, she is likely to feel underutilized, become impatient, and leave. It is truly a balancing act.

Once you finally take the leap, it can be terrifying. There are nights when Letha Pugh, co-owner of Bake Me Happy, a wholesale and retail baking company, lies awake hoping customers will still show up the next day. She and her wife and business partner, Wendy Williams Pugh, employ eighteen workers in Columbus, Ohio. They now own two café storefronts and recently purchased a historic building because they needed a larger kitchen.

The couple launched their business in 2013, when the demand for the gluten-free oatmeal crème cloud cookies and donut muffins Wendy baked in their home kitchen for private clients took off.

Letha was always entrepreneurial. She grew up poor and remembers doing odd jobs around her neighborhood over the weekends to earn a single food stamp that she could take to the drugstore to buy packages of grape and strawberry Now & Laters. On Mondays, when she was bused to a suburban school forty-five minutes away, she would sell the candy to her affluent classmates, marking up the price to earn a profit. Then she would give the cash to her mom to buy dishwashing liquid or toilet paper, household staples her family's food stamp allotment didn't cover. She later put herself through college and nursing school and even ran her own home-health-care agency for a while. Once she saw customers lining up for Wendy's cookies and muffins, she knew they could build something much bigger.

"I said, 'Hey, I don't want to get to the end of my life, and we've had this mom-and-pop bakery and it's good and it works, but there's more. We can do more,'" she recalls telling Wendy.

They started renting space in a shared commercial kitchen and then applied to a small-business incubator geared to founders of color. With guidance from mentors, Letha met new contacts, and she quickly began closing deals to supply gluten-free treats to commercial cafeterias at Chase Bank, Huntington Bank, and then their biggest customer, Ohio State University. With only two bakers, Wendy and another woman who would become their third partner, Bake Me Happy quickly needed more hands to frost enough cupcakes and mix up enough scones to fill new, larger orders. They weren't turning a profit yet, but they needed help in the kitchen to scale. To make it work, Letha deferred a salary until recently. Instead of paying herself, they invested in staff.

When COVID-19 hit and the commercial kitchens Bake Me Happy had supplied closed, wholesale orders suddenly dried up. Letha and Wendy pivoted to selling directly to consumers looking for gluten-free items, and nearly overnight they turned the front of their production kitchen into a retail shop with online ordering and carry-out menu. Through the help of the Goldman Sachs 10,000 Small Businesses program housed at the local community college, they applied and received federal aid to keep their nine full-time and nine part-time staffers on throughout the pandemic. But they kept their operation lean. They couldn't afford a marketing company, so when Wendy isn't baking she creates and posts social media content. They couldn't afford a packaging machine, so when they aren't serving coffee, the staffers who work in the retail coffee shops do the labeling for the wholesale side of the business.

"It's scrappy. And there's not a lot of fluff. But we pay our staff well. We bring in lunch, trying to support other small restaurant businesses . . . a couple of times a month. We have a snack cooler. Whatever we can do . . . we want it to be a good place to work. Our staff is very diverse and we have a lot of long-term staff," Letha told us.

She's found employees who are willing to be flexible and understand that the owners and managers are human too. She looks for hires who are willing to think ahead and go the extra mile. Acting with the team in mind is what sets great employees apart from good employees, and Letha says that despite the labor shortage challenging many small businesses in 2021, she's found great hires.

We lucked out that as we hit our own growth phase, we had recently brought on an intern who immediately added immense value. Brittany Roderick was a Georgia Tech senior whom Lara had met through a class she taught part time in the evenings. What began as an internship for the scholarship athlete quickly turned into several afternoons a week, when she took on any task that needed to be done. No matter how menial or repetitive the job at hand, Brittany was our fail-safe.

We were lucky we didn't scare her off with the frenzy in our Nourish office in early 2010. She joined us just as we launched a spur-of-the-moment charitable program, donating thousands of cases of Nourish to relief efforts in Haiti. The devastating 7.0 earthquake that struck south of Port-au-Prince in late January 2010 left nearly three million people without access to clean drinking water. We felt compelled to help. A parishioner of the church where Lara's son, Connor, attended day care had access to a fleet of planes and had begun mobilizing an emergency mission to deliver supplies, and we immediately offered our water bottles. For every case purchased by our customers, we donated a case. People could also donate cases directly and dedicate them in honor or memory of a loved one or friend. Brittany stood with us for hours with a black Sharpie in hand, scrawling the individual dedications on each box. She crammed cases into her SUV to ferry them to the church to be airlifted to families in need.

The Haiti project was just the beginning. You may recall that the unique shape of our bottles to fit the small hands of babies and children necessitated manual assembly. There were times when it was literally *our* hands doing the work.

If we got a last-minute order, and John Burleson at English

Mountain Spring didn't have enough workers scheduled, we were it. The three of us would road trip to the plant outside Knoxville to spend the day screwing the closures on top of hundreds of baby and toddler bottles. We still smile remembering Brittany in her knee-high rain boots working inside the "clean" room at the plant, where she braved the inevitable splashes and puddles as our bottles were filled with purified water.

The two of us would be just on the other side of the glass-encased room, looking like Lucy and Ethel at the chocolate factory in our hairnets and rubber gloves, pulling the bottles off the conveyor belt and capping them one by one. When she wasn't in the clean room, Brittany was there to help us lug cases by hand or push a dolly piled high to her truck or to Lara's to drive the bottles to Atlanta. Each day, she would pack cases and bring them to UPS or FedEx and make sure they arrived at their intended destination. We truly couldn't have done it all without her energy and sunny outlook. This was all in addition to her invaluable work on our website. She taught herself web design and within six months had built out our online marketing and customer-service division.

As Brittany prepared for commencement in the fall, initially with an eye on a high-paying finance job, we asked if she would come work for us full time. We knew we couldn't offer her a big salary. But what we couldn't offer in cash we could offer in flexibility. She could continue coaching the club volleyball team she loved a few afternoons a week, plus live out her sports-announcing dreams narrating the play-by-play for the Georgia Tech women's volleyball games. We knew if we were going to put anyone on the payroll as a full-time W2 employee of Nourish Corporation, it had to be Brittany. When she graduated, she became the only employee who received a check every two weeks from Nourish Corporation. We certainly didn't.

Finally, we had hired someone who could be patient with our startup journey. More importantly, we could put into practice the lessons we'd learned. Brittany understood from the outset that the workload would outmatch the pay. We had explicit conversations about how the business model operated, and when Brittany would assist Stacey with accounts payable, she got to see firsthand the distance between sales and revenue. We were careful to balance the flashier parts with the grittier realities. Yes, she stood in the bottling factory with us, but we also brought her to awards dinners to celebrate with us. As we expanded, we learned additional lessons together. We had both come from work experiences where customer service took precedence, and Brittany brought a new dimension to our growth. She learned the business well enough to field complaints independently or to navigate thorny issues raised by our retailers. The most sustainable businesses are ones where everyone has skin in the game, and where the high quality of the interaction never wavers. Over the next few years, we brought on part-time contractors or had short-term help, but Brittany symbolized our core learning: The one thing you can never afford to lose are the people buying your stuff, so make their experience the center of your business. Everything else is either fungible or negotiable. Our decision would prove prophetic when we eventually got the chance to pitch Nourish to the one customer we thought we wanted most.

LEVEL-UP LESSONS:
CHAPTER 5

- Resist the urge to hire and raise money from close friends. Your excitement will attract friends who want to help. Friends should not be both investors and employees. As you scale, if you hire friends, they should not report directly to you.

- Hire patience and hire patiently. Scaling a business takes time.

- Hire for mindsets over skill sets. For most positions, you can teach someone to do what you need done, but you cannot teach a person how to think. Be sure your interview process gets at mindsets. Give homework projects to candidates and observe how they approach tasks.

- Hire sales and customer service first. Of the Three Cs of Growth, the first one you have to get is a customer.

6

...

CASH IS KING. BUT FLOW IS QUEEN.

With Stacey running operations while chasing invoices and Brittany making sure deliveries ran smoothly, Lara revved up her engine to land a major new sale. After more than two long years of building solid repeat orders from smaller boutiques and airport shops, we'd also been selling Nourish directly to consumers on Amazon and on our own website. By leveraging our networks, we'd generated national media buzz. With stable revenue (though no profit), we had right-sized and right-selected our staff. Now to revisit an earlier decision. We had decided against a major retailer at launch, but we had found our footing, produced bottles, and proven our supply chain. The next stage in scaling up would be one of the big grocery stores. The time had come.

Chasing the Car

From the start, we envisioned Nourish as an aspirational product for parents who cared about the health and wellness of their little ones. A 2009 feature on the hip baby blog *Daily Candy Kids*, the top read for trendy moms at the time, played to the kind of educated, upscale customer we expected to buy our baby water. With our upmarket price point, due in part to the fact that our bottles were assembled by hand, reaching customers willing to shell out six dollars for a premium product was right on plan and fit our growth model.

We had managed to meet this client profile through baby braithwaite and the hotels and airports that carried our product. However, the grocery store that catered to our target clientele was Whole Foods. Neither of us had a direct connection to the company, but Lara had never met a stranger. As we scoured our list of contacts, we discovered one potential lead. A Canadian small-business owner we met at the All Baby and Child trade show had admired our glossy white-and-green booth at the expo and casually mentioned that Whole Foods carried her products in Canada. We emailed her to see if she could make an introduction. In the meantime, Lara drove to the Whole Foods near her home in Buckhead, and she gamely hit up the store manager for the name of the local Atlanta buyer for the baby category.

Unlike most of the major supermarket chains, Whole Foods relied on regional and local buyers who were on the hunt for hot new products from local purveyors. We learned that the buyers reset the shelf space for a specific category only once a year. The timing had to be right for you to catch them during the period when they would map out their "planogram," a diagram of which products would be sold where. Often the big brands dominated the prime space at eye level, but if Whole Foods was testing out a new line of natural baby food or fair-trade cake mix or organic peanut butter, the buyers would reserve a few lower shelves for them. The trick was to pique their interest at just the right moment. Once Lara had the Atlanta buyer's name and contact information, she diligently emailed and called him to ask if he would consider looking at Nourish, to no avail.

At the same time, we enlisted the help of Lara's friend, Olympic champion volleyball player Holly McPeak. Holly was married to legendary sports agent Leonard Armato, who represented athletes such as Shaquille O'Neal. He had served as chairman of Dunk.net, Shaq's basketball shoe brand, where Lara had worked a decade before. They had stayed in touch, and she and Holly reconnected in person when we went out to L.A. to promote Nourish. Holly, a new mom, had become our de facto team member for West Coast displays and celebrity events. So we were thrilled when she offered to try to track down the local Whole Foods buyer in her area. Eventually she did, and that proved pivotal. Holly got a name for us: Diane Snyder, the buyer responsible for the entire Whole Foods Southern Pacific region, including Southern California, Hawaii, Arizona, and Southern Nevada. We started emailing Diane nonstop. We sent her loads of Nourish bottles and our lime-green swag. There was no way this woman was going to say no to us. We were going to do whatever we could to grab her attention.

After a few months, our persistence paid off. Diane agreed to give Nourish a test with access to at least twenty stores as a store-optional item. But to qualify, we couldn't simply pack up some cases and ship them to the stores. This was the big time. We needed to be accepted by UNFI, United Natural Foods, Inc., the large distributor that would warehouse and transport our water bottles by the truckload to loading docks at Whole Foods across the Southwest. We were also told we would need to engage a broker who would liaise with the retailers and monitor the merchandising. The broker was typically the person who would also approach retailers to sell our product into the target stores. With limited funds and a wariness about adding more layers between us and our customer, we hesitated. Essentially, we would be paying someone to do what we'd already done through Diane. But as Lara's pursuit of the Atlanta buyer had shown, and as Holly's intro proved, who you used mattered. With expansion as a tantalizing prospect, we decided a broker was worth the investment to land the Whole Foods locations. Once we were accepted by UNFI, even with the broker Nourish faced a six-month lag time to get set up in the system. It was another delay, but we were making progress.

Yes . . . but

The day-to-day responsibilities of running Nourish Corporation continued to pick up steam in 2010, as did our outside obligations. Although Stacey spent long hours at the Georgia Capitol voting on bills and answering constituent concerns from January to late March or early April, we stayed in regular touch. Stacey had taken on fundraising responsibilities for the Georgia House Democratic Caucus, and she was becoming more involved in party leadership. Connor was now spending most mornings a week at preschool, so Lara continued her work on the Georgia Regional Transportation Authority (GRTA) board, after serving on the temporary Transit Planning and Transit Implementation boards. She had been appointed to GRTA by Republican governor Sonny Perdue in 2008, and in 2012, Governor Nathan Deal, also a Republican, reappointed her to continue advising the state on transportation projects. Our bipartisan business partnership often caught people by surprise. They asked incredulously how we could possibly work together, or they assumed we just never discussed politics. On the contrary, we love to talk politics. But we have learned to separate politics from our core values. Those we share. The fact that the two of us don't always hold the same point of view on policy is exactly why we have a successful partnership and friendship. We're both smart. We respect each other. If there were times when we disagreed, the response by each of us was often, "Hmm. What does *she* see that *I don't* see?" The fact that we each approach things differently is our superpower. It makes us better problem solvers in business and in life.

Our differing perspectives came into play as we continued to grow the volume of our business, including the pending deal with Whole Foods. One of us was ready to sign up for a full slate of options right away, while the other cautioned we needed to slow down and read the fine print. Bet you can guess who said, "Yes," and who said, "But . . ." Whole Foods had presented us with a substantive layout of the terms for accessing their shelves. Conditions included how long we would extend them credit to pay us for our products after we shipped them, what marketing programs we could pay to participate in, and what deductions could be taken if mistakes happened on our end, like a label placed on the wrong side of a box or a shipment arriving outside the assigned window for delivery. These provisions were familiar from some other customers, but this was in a whole new league. Luckily, Matt Hughes had been a trusted resource when we first set up our supply chain, and he knew the retail terrain well. He offered to help us navigate this mountain of verbiage.

Over a tall hot chocolate for Stacey and a frothy whipped cream topped Frappuccino for Lara, we parked ourselves at the Starbucks on Peachtree Road over several mornings, poring over the paperwork with Matt. We had gotten used to our smaller clients already delaying payment for our products and had managed to scrape by when they didn't pay us on time. Stacey had worked accounts payable calls into her regular routine. We just figured this was the cost of doing business. Yet this would be the first time we would be dealing with a huge national retailer and with invoices that had more zeroes than ever before. If we wanted to go for it, we knew we would have to accept the net 30 terms on paper, agreeing that Whole Foods could take thirty days to pay us after we shipped the products, and be prepared for the possibility we might wait longer than thirty days for payment. We suspected thirty days was an intention, not a promise. Between marketing fees, supply chain obligations, and other items that made Whole Foods unique, Matt helped us sift through what saying yes would mean.

Despite our combined experience in corporate dealmaking and the law, the contract was daunting—but we couldn't take forever to judge the costs versus the benefits. This is one of the tough balancing acts of being an entrepreneur. On the one hand, you need to be intentional and deliberate with big decisions, knowing that your choices affect not just the bottom line but future opportunities. On the other side of the calculus, if someone's ready to buy your stuff, you feel like you better get it done. Anything can happen to change the circumstances and conditions, and time is what kills most deals. In the end, despite our concerns about when we would get paid, we signed on and got to the business of making it work out.

Capital Crunch Ahead

Cash flow was already weighing on us. We were running a lean operation and didn't have much in reserve. We weren't paying ourselves yet, only Brittany and our temporary contractors. Instead, we signed agreements with the company that allowed us to accrue salary with no hope of being paid until we were squarely in the black. This had two effects. One, both of us had to continue to generate revenue in other ways, Stacey writing and serving in the legislature and Lara accepting speaking gigs. We still took on the occasional Insomnia client, but Nourish came first. The days of floating the company needed to end.

Because we had agreed to extended payment terms with other smaller customers, we were getting behind on our payments to the suppliers who manufactured our components, filled our bottles, and designed our marketing materials—all small businesses too. Once we took on Whole Foods with increasingly larger orders to follow, the amount we would owe our suppliers and our vendors would grow, because we would be spending more to support the larger orders. When our small invoices were late, we could cover them with our own capital if needed. However, if the larger invoices were late, we could not pay our suppliers. Because they had their own obligations and employees to support, eventually they would stop supplying us. Everyone knows the old saying: "Cash is king." But we were quickly figuring out that *flow* is queen. Without ongoing *cash flow*, you're destined to run out of the fuel for business: commerce and customers.

All we needed, we thought, was more time. This is why one afternoon, we drove an hour south to Newnan, a charming city in the metro Atlanta area and the headquarters of Commercial Plastic Composites. The small machine shop produced the silicon closures for our bottles, and we owed the company a modest but not insignificant amount for prior orders. Our plan was to sit down with the owner, a genteel white-haired gentleman named Van Pell, and share our promising news about Whole Foods. We planned to assure him we would work hard to keep up with the outstanding bills, but we simply needed a little longer grace period. We had our updated deck and current spreadsheets ready to go.

Van was one of the most financially sophisticated small-business owners we had encountered. He had a Harvard MBA and had spent a career working in capital markets and real estate development. The machine shop was a second act that provided a convenient income stream while he and his wife enjoyed the mild Georgia winters and the nearby lake. As we settled into the two armchairs across from Van's large desk, we earnestly told him about the delay we were experiencing in receiving payments from many of our customers, and we also shared the payment terms of the upcoming Whole Foods orders, insisting that as soon as our customers paid us, we would make him whole.

He looked at us knowingly and replied, "Nobody gets paid in thirty days."

Of course, we had experienced that firsthand with our smaller customers, but we'd hoped a large company wouldn't be as tight with cash.

Then he went on, eyes crinkling behind wire-rimmed glasses as he shared a pearl of wisdom. "You two have a working capital issue. Everybody has that."

Hearing Van articulate it so starkly relieved some of the embarrassment we felt coming to ask for a favor and an extension. Both of us liked to meet our debts, and we never forgot that we were stewards for friends and family that had invested in us. Although ongoing negotiations with suppliers and assiduous pleas to retailers had become part of our daily lives, Van's statement made us feel less alone. Small-business owners everywhere were struggling with the same concerns. This wasn't an issue of smarts or work ethic; it was a capital issue that we had failed to bake into our planning. Van assured us that he understood where we were in the growth cycle, and that like every other small-business owner out there, we should turn to a bank.

You'll remember that we had resisted borrowing from a lender early on because we weren't in a position to make personal guarantees. He told us to reconsider applying for a line of credit with our bank to help bridge the gap between payments. He also told us about a third party to whom we could sell unpaid invoices. We knew about the business tactic of factoring from business school and law school. Now, as business owners, theory gave way to reality. If we used the service, the factor would chase down the debts for us while advancing a portion of the cash we were owed. The catch was that we could end up shouldering high interest rates and possibly having to pay the debt and interest ourselves if the original charges didn't get settled. Factoring enjoyed an uneven reputation because of the risk and some of the less savory companies that offered the service. Most business owners saw their financing option as a last resort.

Like all advice, we decided it didn't hurt to investigate. Factoring— on its face—seemed tailor-made for our challenge. We had invoices from multiple clients and we had stock. What we didn't have was the cash both promised. With the wheels turning in our heads, we left Newnan and Van promising to do our homework. We had to start searching for ways to get cash flowing into Nourish, sooner rather than later.

Researching how to get more working capital became one more thing to add to our ever-longer to-do list for Nourish. It was hard some days just to get through the workload that was already piling up. But just as we had with Insomnia Consulting, we'd fallen into a groove that accommodated our busy schedules. Sometimes it meant emailing between legislative committee hearings or doing calls in our cars while racing to a meeting or pickup at day care or catching up with each other in the evenings in one of our living rooms after a long day. In keeping with our mutual night-owl habits, when the legislature was in session, Stacey focused on Nourish after hours.

Overnight she would take care of any writing or editing we needed, review contracts, and handle the "dunning" side of the business. Dunning letters are the stern communiqués you send to customers when payments are past due, and this was something she could do even if it was past midnight. We worried that those dunning letters were beginning to pile up. Would we have to send one to Whole Foods at some point? And would we even dare after we had worked so hard to break in?

Listen Up and Let Go

Brittany, our one and only full-time employee, was our direct link to customers. She oversaw the Nourish website and replied to inquiries and occasional complaints. If there was a problem with a damaged shipment or someone asked a question on social media, Brittany responded on our behalf. She visited local shops that carried Nourish and reported back to us on whether the store had our inventory in stock. She was the person on the front lines making sure customers were happy. She also became our eyes and ears on the ground with our supply chain. We tried hard to make her feel that she could share her observations with us.

This was a key learning for us. Starting out, you tend to think of customers only as the entity buying your product. But your customers are also your channel partners because they influence how your end customer, the consumer, will experience the product. Getting insights from store owners and those who interacted with our end customers was incredibly valuable. In addition to your channel partners, who distribute your product, and your customers, stake-holders are also part of your ecosystem. Businesses you work with who supply your inventory; vendors who deliver services such as marketing, packaging, and shipping; anybody who relies on you, or you rely on, like Van Pell at Commercial Plastic Composites, are also stakeholders you have to satisfy and who impact your cus-tomer. We discovered that a business operates in a complex net-work and any weak node of the system can affect the success of your business, so you have to pay attention to the needs of all stake-holders. Often the needs of various stakeholders can conflict with one another. For example, Commercial Plastic Composites con-tacted us to let us know that the supply chain for our raw materials was getting stretched and their suppliers were no longer maintain-ing inventory on hand, which meant that it would take longer for our next order to arrive. Their suppliers were now requiring an up-front payment, which would put financial pressure on them, so we would have to get orders in sooner and pay faster, at the very time when our customers wanted longer to pay. We were literally being stretched on both sides by the indirect forces in our eco-system.

Brittany was instrumental in processing the ways we needed to make the website more user-friendly. She helped us become a better business as we continued to expand. We realized there are points in our growth when we could be growing faster if we had more insight into how the business was running. Or we could make improvements if only someone would advise which changes were necessary or wise. If our staff didn't feel comfortable telling us what we needed to know, that would impede our growth. How could we solve problems that weren't articulated? We made sure Brittany felt empowered to solve customer and stakeholder problems on the spot. Sometimes that meant offering a refund to a client or running a new shipment over because of delays in transit. For more complex issues, she turned to us, but we encouraged her to bring us not only problems but also her ideas. On car trips with Lara to suppliers, she learned about how we thought through production challenges and imagined next steps. In the office, we discussed amortization schedules and how to edit marketing materials to succinctly but effectively catch a customer's attention. Most important for us, we involved her in finding solutions. We would regularly go through what she had heard in interactions with clients and vendors, and discuss how to address issues at hand and how to prevent the same issues from reoccurring. When both of our outside obligations mounted, we had to allow Brittany to take the initiative with customers and partners. At times, we felt out of the loop and would try to reinsert ourselves, but then we became the bottleneck. We learned that our focus should not always be on finding answers, but rather on finding the right questions to ask and empowering Brittany to develop solutions.

Focus on Impact

The other thing we took away during this scaling phase was that as founders, we had to become more comfortable really listening to the people closest to our products. A startup founder is really close to the customer. Maybe you are the customer, because you designed your product for yourself. But as the business grows, you become more removed. Customers are the real barometers of effectiveness. If they offer feedback to your frontline employees but you refuse to listen, then the company will stagnate or die. This is an emotional hurdle for founders that limits their companies' growth. The best founders grow *with* their creations and understand that distance is good. The ability to evaluate from a posture of leadership versus ownership means having a flexible mindset and sometimes the willingness to let go of your original vision to create space for a better one.

Most entrepreneurs are naturally passionate about "what" they do, and their ego is wrapped up in their product. When a customer suggests possible improvements, it's natural to get defensive about your product and not really listen. The key to scaling your business is to be sure your ego and your passion are invested in the *impact* of the product. Then, you are all ears when someone suggests an improvement.

Helya Mohammadian unexpectedly scrapped the entire marketing plan for her innovative side-fastening underwear. The pitch was initially aimed at new moms who couldn't pull up typical panties following a C-section procedure. When she launched a Kickstarter campaign to finance the first batch, she discovered she was missing out on an entirely different group of consumers. Wheelchair users, people with chronic illnesses and their caregivers, and women who lived with catheters or ports and all types of mobility issues reached out, sharing their stories about why they needed adaptive underwear. Helya suddenly realized there was a much bigger market for her company, Slick Chicks. She wasn't familiar with adaptive clothing made for people with physical challenges when she first started out, but suddenly she understood how her product could serve many more people.

"It really opened my eyes and I was changed by it. The product didn't change 100 percent, but we definitely made some iterations. And we pivoted our messaging and made sure we were clear with our mission," she told us.

She had to let go of the postpartum women she envisioned as her main customer base and think differently about the product line. The switch wasn't easy, but it made Slick Chicks stand out and ultimately helped Helya grab the attention of an investor who has become her biggest champion and mentor. Eight years after starting her company, the underwear is now sold at Target and JCPenney.

"Looking back on it, it was the best thing I could ever have done. Listening to those first customers put a lot of things in perspective for me," she says.

For Nourish, Brittany facilitated real-time feedback with our customers and our suppliers. She was the one who first alerted us that some of the initial cases we sent to Whole Foods were damaged. We were charged penalties for the broken shipments. We needed to figure out what went wrong, so we dispatched Brittany to the English Mountain plant in Tennessee to diagnose the problem. When she arrived, she saw that the cases were packed in square boxes and then loaded onto pallets. Instead of interlocking for stability, they were sliding off the pallets as soon as the shrink-wrap was removed by the buyers at Whole Foods. We didn't waste time assigning blame. We just needed to fix the mechanics and move ahead. Thanks to Brittany, we changed the packaging from square boxes to rectangles that could be crisscrossed like Lincoln Logs.

She also fielded emails from UNFI and Whole Foods, including inquiries from local buyers asking for "free-fills." We had no idea what they meant. So we called Matt Hughes, and we learned that along with the order for a certain number of cases, individual stores often expected a freebie, aka a free extra case of products. Once again, we learned this was the cost of doing business with a big retailer and keeping the customer happy.

By November 2010, trucks had begun driving the first cases from our little Southeast hub across the country to UNFI, and on to Whole Foods markets from Scottsdale to San Diego. With some trepidation but with insights from Van, we had signed on with an Atlanta factoring company called FTRANS to help us bridge our cash-flow needs. We remained hopeful they could service the larger Whole Foods invoices. Our immediate focus had to be getting Nourish out the door and on time. All this coincided with Staccy winning a historic election to lead the Democrats in the Georgia House of Representatives. She would become the first woman to lead either party in the General Assembly, and the first person of color to serve as House minority leader.

Things appeared to be falling into place. But growth also meant we were past the point where Brittany could simply load up her SUV and drop off the cases at FedEx. Nourish was on the verge of outgrowing English Mountain's manual assembly line, too, as we would get orders requiring us to fill, pack, and ship thousands of bottles with just a few days' notice. We needed to automate production and fill and seal more bottles faster. That meant investing in a new piece of equipment to secure the closures on the bottles. Hand closure, where a staff member physically affixed the cap, meant paying for each person. But it also meant that we had to know our orders well in advance. Between Whole Foods and our other clients, we couldn't always predict our inventory needs. The manual process was both expensive and hard to schedule at the last minute. Standard capping equipment was made to screw small standard caps onto a typical bottle of water, but it could not screw our closures, which included a collar with the sippy or nipple top covered by a protective cap. The new capping equipment would cost at least $150,000. We figured out how to raise half of that, but the rest eluded us.

Thirty days came and went after shipping the first cases out West to Whole Foods. Christmas approached, but the first big check never arrived. We called UNFI daily to get an ETA on the payment and were told, over and over, without fail, some version of "the payment is in process" or "the check is in the mail."

LEVEL-UP LESSONS:
CHAPTER 6

- Cash is king, but flow is queen, and you can't win a chess match without flow. Borrowing or raising money does not create flow. Even if you borrow money to keep the business going, don't forget that you need to address the problem of cash flow.

- You don't know what you don't know. Focus on finding the right questions over finding answers.

- Time kills all deals. Don't let perfect get in the way of progress.

- Focus on impact over product when receiving feedback. What matters is how your product helps, not simply how it works. If your ego is invested in the particulars of your product's manufacturing or aesthetics, you'll miss valuable feedback about its impact and even opportunities for growth.

- Let go as you grow. Ensure your frontline team members have a way to communicate unfiltered feedback.

- Do not play the blame game. Focus on solutions and move on.

- The biggest bottleneck to growth is often the founder. You can do most things, and likely have over time, but that does not mean you should do all of them.

7

GROWING OUT
OF BUSINESS

n 2010, we finally caught the car. We had achieved the dream we had relentlessly chased down for close to four years: Nourish was finally on the shelves of a national grocery retailer. Weekly orders were coming in from multiple Amazon distribution centers and from Paradies shops across the U.S., and parents were snapping up our water bottles for their babies and kids. The business finally felt like it was hitting its stride, with recurring orders and six-figure revenue. But we had learned that although we were expected to deliver our products on time to stores, our clients operated by a different, well-established set of payment rules. The glory of getting larger customers and larger orders didn't produce a windfall. Instead, we confronted the age-old mismatch between small-business owner cash flow and major-corporation financing. Our grocery retailer's invoices were taking close to four months to be paid. That's sixty to ninety days past due on a net 30 invoice. As we waited longer and longer to get paid, we dug ourselves deeper into debt with our suppliers. We needed working capital, and we needed it now.

Credit Crunch Hits Home

The timing couldn't have been worse. The nation's anemic recovery from the 2008 financial crisis continued to take its toll on homeowners and small businesses alike. The Treasury Department's Capital Purchase Program, which injected $200 billion into more than nine hundred banks in hopes of stimulating loans to Main Street, had stumbled. Instead of boosting lending, the banks that received government aid *decreased* business loans even more than banks that didn't get the funds, according to a sobering 2012 analysis by the SBA. From 2008 to 2011, small-business lending dropped by 18 percent, as banks tightened credit requirements on applicants and regulators pressured banks to conserve capital and make less risky loans.

In addition, many of the smaller banks that survived the financial meltdown were gobbled up by the giant banking conglomerates and closed, leaving poor and rural parts of the country altogether without neighborhood banks. Community banks once made the majority of loans to small firms. Without them, entrepreneurs could no longer rely on the trusted personal relationships they had built with the bankers they would see at church or on Back-to-School

Night—people who knew the ins and outs of the businesses. These local connections had been the bedrock of small business in America for generations, and they had evaporated at the worst possible time. This was the uncertain landscape in which we set out to secure a lifeline for Nourish.

The national credit crunch was just one of the reasons we ran into an obstacle we didn't expect while trying to raise capital at this stage in our business. Even though we could demonstrate recurring revenue, increasing sales, and forecast cash flow from our outstanding invoices, our national bank still wanted us to provide personal guarantees for a loan. The bank was a "cash-flow lender," meaning that it looked first at the pace of revenue and expenses of the business to be sure Nourish was taking in sufficient funds regularly to pay the loan back. See the irony here? You need a loan because of uncertain cash flow but you need certain cash flow to get the loan. If your books don't show you can cover the loan, the bank looks to your personal assets. Our only real assets were our modest homes, and neither of us could justify putting them up as collateral.

Using your personal credit to finance your business is one of the unseen hurdles that stifles growth for many small-business owners. The expectation is counterintuitive and mind-boggling. When you start a business, best practices say to keep your business and personal accounts separate and never to commingle your money. Stories of bootstrapping by tapping into your house's equity sound exciting and even doable—unless you have real obligations at home. The quality of your business model and the strength of your execution should be what matters—not the size of your mortgage. But what we learned is that institutional lenders throw this smart practice out the window when your business needs a loan. If you don't have the independent wealth to own a home or a big investment portfolio, or if you are paying down school loans or have a lower credit score because you've struggled financially at times, you are out of luck. This insistence on risking personal ruin to improve your cash flow cuts out a huge number of small-business owners from ever accessing capital from banks. In our case, we could look at our outstanding invoices and know the money was out there. We could also look at our homes and weigh the risk of personal guarantees. But we couldn't put the security of our families on the financial line. Without the personal guarantee, we'd hit another wall. We didn't have three months or more to wait for our bank to process the application only to be denied anyway. We needed the money so we could scale now.

Easy Money Is Never Easy

Our friend Marie Hunter could relate to our frustrations. The president and CEO of KRG Oil in Atlanta spent three years trying to secure a line of credit from her bank to keep pace with the growth of her company, only to be turned down when she needed capital most. Her business provides wholesale bulk fuel purchases to contractors, hotels, and hospitals. But as she signed on larger clients, to remain competitive KRG had to offer extended payment options, and that slowed down her cash flow.

She experimented with factoring, as we had. But the high fees on each outstanding invoice added up fast every day that the debt wasn't settled. Factoring wasn't the only alternative she tried. A proliferation of new online lending options began to entice entrepreneurs when credit dried up after 2008. A Federal Reserve report found that by 2018, a third of small businesses were applying for financing through these emerging vehicles. While the loan approval rates by the lenders were higher than traditional banks, the terms and associated costs were often gravely misunderstood by entrepreneurs who struggled with high interest rates along with confusing and often unfavorable repayment terms.

Marie experienced exactly this when she was approved for a loan from a small-business lender. Lara remembers a tearful phone call in which Marie confided that even though her commercial customers paid her weekly, the arrangement with the fintech company allowed it to take money directly out of her business checking account every single day to repay the loan. Even though on paper the loan didn't look expensive, its structure was entirely wrong for her situation and much more costly than it initially appeared.

The lending companies don't know the intimate details of your business and they don't care. They just want to make a loan. And if you don't understand your numbers clearly enough to steer clear of traps like these, that's a recipe for disaster. Always look for hidden pricing. There can be fees for everything from an early payment on a loan to auto-withdrawals from your bank account from online lenders, as Marie encountered. Never let someone take your money themselves. If they don't trust you to give it to them, don't work with that lender. Only *you* should move money from your account.

Although Nourish didn't go down the road of using an online lender, we did experiment with alternative debt financing when we enlisted the help of FTRANS and bank-sponsored factoring. Heading in, we understood the risks from an academic perspective, but direct experience is quite the teacher. Factoring requires constant monitoring of inventory as well as an unsettling level of uncertainty. For some businesses and industries, this is accepted practice. As a small manufacturing business on the hook to suppliers and customers, factoring was an imperfect solution that could not solve all our cash-flow needs.

Bottom line: Not all capital is equal. What Marie faced was a financial shell game. Lenders like that count on clients who are not financially savvy and, sadly, are perceived as high risk in order to justify the usury terms. Nourish had a separate challenge. Factoring generally depends on high-volume transactions, so businesses that cannot meet the obligations put their companies in jeopardy with every order. Bank loans are the safest source, on paper, though they may require personal guarantees, as we've discussed. But the traditional banking relationship no longer exists for most. It costs a bank roughly the same amount to process a $25,000 loan as it does to process a $250,000 application. For the business owner trying to cover cash-flow issues, the twin threats are (1) being too small to get the loan, or (2) taking out too much and losing even more. Every day, though, business owners riffle through their credit cards looking for one with a little more give, and they hunt the internet for a payment solution that promises to solve the capital imbalance.

While we are critical of the capital financing systems as they currently exist, we understand the fundamental reality facing small businesses that can't afford to wait for wholesale change. We couldn't. That's why we caution that every capital solution comes with a cost, and you have to understand how each one works in order to make sure you don't sign up with the wrong one. This seems self-evident, but panic can make us blind to warning signs. When you look at the terms, you must remember that the cost of doing business should not *be your business*. Financing your company should not leave you in a weaker position than when you started.

After doing our homework, we had signed up to use the factoring services of FTRANS to avoid the risk of a retail customer not paying. We had already been stiffed by several boutique stores that placed orders at a trade show and never paid us after receiving the product. More broadly, large retailers who seemed stable, like Circuit City or Toys"R"Us, went out of business and left their suppliers holding the bag. While we could survive a boutique not paying for a few cases, we could not afford to take a loss if a large retailer didn't pay. Yet our proactive steps to protect against defaults fell short. Soon after we'd signed up with FTRANS, they adjusted their underwriting criteria and would not approve our invoices to some of our large customers like Paradies. In the midst of the credit crisis, despite our orders and inventory, we appeared too high risk. The solution we thought would be our salvation turned us away.

Outrunning the Snowball

We were scrambling. On the outside, it looked like we were making it work. But Nourish faced a looming financial crisis, and our suppliers were feeling the pinch too. Every day that we weren't paid by our customers, we couldn't pay the folks producing our merchandise.

Lara pleaded with our manufacturers. "Just make a few more. They're going to pay us. Just make a few more, can we do a little bit more?" Stacey cajoled our customers. "Can you pay us by credit card? Even a good-faith payment would do. Can I speak to someone else in accounts receivable?" To no avail. We were trying to outrun the snowball hurtling down the mountain and gaining speed, barely staying a step ahead of being crushed. At some point, it would catch up.

One morning in April 2011, we got a call that truly knocked the wind out of us. John Burleson, the kind owner of English Mountain Spring, had bad news. He and his filling plant just couldn't keep working with us. Our orders were too big for his small operation to continue to do manually. In the back of our minds, we had expected this call would come at some point; still, we were speechless. Panic set in. We started frantically going through all our contacts and sifting through old emails, wondering who we could possibly call to get us out of this jam.

Losing English Mountain had a host of consequences. John and his team had been willing to hand-assemble our bottles *and* understood the delay in payments. Now, we would have to move our bottling operations to a larger filler at the exact moment we learned that Whole Foods wanted more of our bottles. We would have to find a new filler that wouldn't mind manually screwing on thousands of caps to our custom-shaped bottles. We scrambled to find a partner that was larger, and, ideally, one that had more automation we could use. While we were wishing for miracles, we added to the list a vendor closer to Atlanta.

In a bit of serendipity, our network came to the rescue again.

Lara remembered a woman who had written about Nourish for the stylish parenting blog *Daily Candy Kids*. She'd told us that her mother's family owned a pure water spring in southeast Georgia. One year earlier, she had emailed us to ask if we could tell them the company we had used to do our branding and website. We'd been happy to help. This loose connection in mind, Lara called her and arranged a meeting that week. Like we had all those years ago when we went to Tennessee, the two of us embarked on yet another road trip adventure in hopes of finding a solution.

When we arrived at the bucolic home of the deep quartzite water spring that feeds the Callaway Blue bottling operation, our spirits began to rise. Nestled in the rolling hills of Harris County, not far from the verdant hiking trails of F. D. Roosevelt State Park, Callaway Blue seemed to fit the bill. Once we toured the plant, we saw for ourselves that the family-run operation could handle much larger orders than English Mountain could. It also provided the forklifts and commercial loading docks that Nourish now required, as shipping companies transported our product directly to the distributor's facility.

We struck a deal with the owners on the spot, and they agreed to start right away so we could be ready for the next Whole Foods order. We scrambled to move our inventory of parts from English Mountain to the Callaway Blue Spring Water Company. The new filler ticked almost every box but one. While Callaway Blue could help us boost the number of bottles filled and shipped, we still needed to rely on manual labor because their high speed line could not yet accommodate our unique bottles. They had plans to expand

and thought they could meet our needs. Yet we knew that assembling the bottles by hand would not be feasible for much longer. We needed cash to buy the right machinery to automate as soon as possible. We had to find a way to finance it.

VC Isn't a Meritocracy

Although we were a bit gun-shy going back to venture investors to try to raise equity after we had previously been rebuffed, we reasoned that Nourish was in a much more attractive position than when we first pitched our concept several years before. We also felt we could raise venture capital without giving away too much ownership since we had revenue, we had Whole Foods, and perhaps there would be other big customers like Kroger and Walgreens on the horizon. Unlike our first go-round courting outside investors in 2007, Nourish was now a real company with actual revenue, not a startup that hadn't proved its mettle. On paper, our company possessed all the right qualities to attract equity investors. Nourish had solid demand and a buzzy story, or in Silicon Valley lingo, "product market fit." We owned a patented design, meaning we had successfully registered our distinct concept with the U.S. Patent Office, making the intellectual property defensible if someone tried to copy our style. Unlike in 2008, we had solid proof of concept that the design worked and was feasible, and most importantly, we were in conversations with other large retailers to expand into hundreds of retail locations if we could level up and expand production.

As a startup manufacturing business, we had hit all the targets financiers told us to aim for—and we'd done so with a tight circle of investors and scrappy development. Our company had won awards for our concept, and major players had become our premiere customers. Across a host of metrics, we had met or exceeded expectations, and now we simply needed the funds to automate and to expand our marketing to a broader audience. We painstakingly refined our deck, researched likely investors, and hunted for comparables to ease any worry about market share. But once again our aggressive and validated pitch didn't get us very far. Nourish still wasn't a hot tech startup, and it wouldn't be able to achieve—or convincingly promise—the "hockey stick" growth most VCs wanted to see.

Louisville serial entrepreneur and investor Paul Ford went through the same journey. When he began pitching VCs on his artificial intelligence–powered insurance data startup, OrchestraRx, his business was already netting $2 million annually and on track to grow to between $10 million and $20 million within three years. But the rosy projection wasn't big enough for the private equity and venture funds he tried to attract to help the company scale. Not even close.

"If you don't say the B word when you first meet a VC, they will not talk to you. And the B word is *billion*," says Paul, underscoring his dismay that investors weren't impressed by the company's solid profits and the five employees on the payroll. They only wanted to know how fast it could grow in value.

Paul was so disillusioned by the experience that in 2018, he launched DS9 Capital, a portfolio management company that purchases intellectual property in insurance tech and incubates new companies founded by diverse entrepreneurs. He counts Ursula Burns, the former chairwoman of the Xerox Corporation and the first Black female CEO of a Fortune 500 company, as one of his investors and mentors. He is working to build a new ecosystem for entrepreneurs of color to find capital and coaching to overcome the roadblocks he encountered himself.

Although we knew that successfully raising venture funding is rare for most companies, we didn't want to admit that we were perhaps experiencing some of the bias (gender, racial, industry sector) present in legacy VC. Male founders were more than three times as likely as female founders to access equity financing through angels or VCs (14.4 percent versus 3.6 percent). The bitter irony that chilled us most was that we were exactly what the VC funders professed to be on the lookout for—we simply didn't look like what they wanted. Years later, the numbers continue to remain equally dismal for Black and Latinx founders. Despite a renewed focus on racial inequality spurred by the Black Lives Matter movement in the summer of 2020, Black and Latinx founders raised just 2.6 percent of VC in the first ten months of 2020.

Level Up or Die

We continued to pitch angel investors and venture funds through the spring of 2011, but our hopes waned. Again and again, we had excellent meetings, got glowing feedback, and then heard nothing but silence. All the while, unpaid invoices competed for dominance with unpaid bills. The dueling rounds of dunning and being dunned were taking their toll. We sat in the office where Stacey maintained shelves labeled "Accounts Payable" and "Accounts Receivable." The fluorescent lights clearly showed that we were owed more than we were taking in on a daily basis. Whole Foods continued to order from us, but they had a luxury we did not. Our suppliers couldn't wait any longer to get paid. Nourish was on life support, and even though we weren't emotionally ready to pull the plug, we knew that's where we were heading.

We continued to update the team that had been with us from the beginning, stalwarts who worked hard for our success. Van Pell, who owned the plastics company that made our closures, and Scott Curlee, who handled our packaging, got regular reports that seemed like death-watch notices. The Callaway family, our new filler, joined the list of those who got our apologies and promises. Desperate to solve our problem, we revisited the idea of personal guarantees and bank loans. But the math didn't work. A loan for a company our size, whose only major asset was a specialized mold, would be a short-term fix. Throw in our homes as collateral and we could borrow enough to last a few more months. Our growth from a dining-room table to a major retailer meant that we had moved too far past the time when $150,000 sufficed. As we look back, the structural impediments Nourish faced with slow payments pre-saged our impasse: steady cash flow, not capacity or even creativity, determined destiny.

After yet another VC rejection, we had to call it. We reached out to the small group of friends and family who believed in our idea from the very beginning and seeded Nourish with their own money and told them that without the ability to raise the funds to automate or expand, Nourish had very little hope of future growth. We would continue to fill orders for customers as long as we had stock, and we would continue to chase unpaid invoices until we could settle our debts. One part they rarely tell you is that while a dream may die, the work continues.

We also realized that sometimes holding on to what you have blinds you to the next opportunity. Sometimes the best ideas are right in front of you.

LEVEL-UP LESSONS: CHAPTER 7

- More businesses *grow* out of business than *go* out of business. Build in extra time and flexibility as you plan for the future. It will probably take longer and more money than you think.

- It is an inconvenient truth that you often need cash flow to borrow money to help with cash flow. A circular argument for sure! Break the circular argument. Get your cash flow from customers and suppliers. Get up-front deposits and accept credit cards. Then you can borrow money for things like inventory, equipment, and hiring.

- Not all dollars are equal. A dollar of equity is more expensive than a dollar of debt, and a dollar of debt is more expensive than a dollar of cash flow from operations or revenue. Cost is not just the number next to the dollar sign. The greatest cost can be the wrong structure, which restricts and does not match your business. Unregulated online lenders look fast and cheap but are not tailored to your business and can even kill it when the loan structure doesn't match your situation.

- The cost of doing business should not be your business! When someone tells you, "That is the cost of doing business," question it. Ask why. Don't let the fear of looking naive or pushy stop you from asking questions that might save your business.

- Venture capital is not a meritocracy. VCs tend to have a herd mentality and will focus on what is "hot" in the market. If you are not in that space, don't pretend to be. Find an investor who likes your space.

- When something fails, mourn and then move on. The next opportunity is around the corner.

8

⋮

LEVEL UP NOW

Insomnia Consulting had continued operations throughout the life of Nourish, providing us with personal income and the means to pay Brittany and occasionally cover our bills. We took on fewer clients, but our reputation as innovative thinkers kept us afloat. After all, our two-woman show had tackled desalination technology, conversions of old quarries, the movement of zinc during an Alaskan winter, and waste-by-rail transfer stations. However, it was during our hunt for financing that we hit upon our next venture.

John Hayes, a former securities attorney, was the founder and chairman of FTRANS, the factoring company that had been part of our growth. With the financial crisis spreading, FTRANS's service model changed too. Van Pell, who'd introduced us to FTRANS, reached out to ask us to meet with John as they explored new ways to guarantee they could serve customers who were suddenly considered risky by the credit market, despite solid performance. Nourish had experienced this when Paradies had been kicked off as a vendor. This was a spreading challenge given the credit environment; since 2009, entire industries had been downgraded, and start-ups like Nourish got caught in the wave of rejections. The banks wanted more security, thus FTRANS really had nothing to market to companies like ours.

At the same time, we were pondering a similar notion. We had followed seasoned advice, filled out reams of paperwork, and delivered product to an array of clients. Yet we were still struggling to survive.

One day, we headed across Peachtree Road to Café Lapin, a French bistro near our offices. As we ordered our salads and sandwiches, we lamented the strange conundrum neither of us had foreseen. Selling our product had been our holy grail—remember, customers + commerce = capital. But we hadn't known that waiting for the capital could take so long. The restaurant never had to experience that delay. At the end of our meal, we'd be handed a list of what we'd ordered, and the price for the meal. Neither of us would hesitate to remit immediate payment, and it wouldn't occur to us to negotiate payment terms for lunch like Wimpy from the Popeye cartoon, who regularly offered to pay Tuesday for a hamburger today.

Both parties understood the transaction. Then there was the payment method. While we were paying the restaurateurs today, the money wouldn't come out of *our* bank accounts until later because we would hand the waiter our credit cards. When the cashier rang up our purchase, the transaction would be approved and Café Lapin would receive an instant infusion of capital.

The restaurant had no accounts receivable. They didn't just recognize their revenue, they actually received it. They wouldn't borrow money for working capital. They wouldn't factor our curry chicken salad or grilled pimento cheese sandwich. No one sat in the back room tabulating financing for our sweet teas. In fact, their business probably rarely involved a bank (except to finance the acquisition of a building or to build out the space). Café Lapin got its due immediately, even though we wouldn't pay our credit card bills for another twenty to thirty days. And if we didn't pay then, the credit card issuer wasn't going to the bistro to take their money back.

Separately, then together, we and John wondered why there wasn't a similar tool for businesses that served other businesses—a method of financing that operated like the credit card to help them get paid faster. Stacey's favorite customers for Nourish were those who used credit cards to buy product directly from our website. We got our money right away from those folks, but our commercial customers wouldn't pay us that way. Lara had gone back to Whole Foods and asked them to pay us with a credit card, but they refused. If they paid us with a credit card, they would owe the bank, and when the bill came due they would have to pay by the deadline or be charged interest and penalties. But if they didn't pay *our* "net 30" invoice in thirty days, nothing would happen. We were their free bank.

Davids and Goliaths

Working with John, we decided to unravel a problem that transcended Nourish and bedeviled FTRANS. The more we investigated, we found story after story about businesses caught in our same quandary over late payments. Not theirs—their customers'.

The National Federation of Independent Business found that 64 percent of the small businesses it surveyed in 2011 reported that their invoices went unpaid for at least sixty days, and delinquencies were getting worse. To add insult to injury, there is no recourse for small businesses like ours when big corporations and government agencies prolong the time they take to pay us. Unlike small companies, Coca-Cola's or Microsoft's credit rating won't be dinged when they don't remit to suppliers on time, whereas a small business that doesn't keep up with its bills gets punished with late fees and a tarnished credit rating. This is because they play under different rules. Small businesses are rated by D&B, Experian, and Equifax for the timeliness of trade and credit card payments. Large companies are rated by the S&P, Moody's, or Fitch on their ability to service their bond debt.

It became clear to us that the reason our biggest customers didn't use a credit card to pay us is that it was to their advantage to delay the payment. Every time a small company makes a big sale, it becomes an indentured *lender* to these giants because it has delivered the good or service and is allowing the customer to hold their money and use it for free. And there is no way around it. You feel like you can't say no. Those are the terms of the sale. It is the "cost of doing business." As an entrepreneur, you really don't think about it because you're so wedded to this model that you just wait to be paid.

Small companies need big customers to purchase more products, yet to make more products (or serve bigger clients), they need cash as soon as possible to pay their expenses. Without that capital, many of us go looking to borrow the money from a bank, only to be told we don't qualify, or we must make a personal guarantee for the loan. It's no wonder that CB Insights found in 2014 that more than a third of small businesses fail because they simply run out of money.

Or, if they don't run out of money, they are doomed to stay small. This is what happened initially to our friend Alisa Clark, CEO of Glory Professional Cleaning Services. Alisa is a force of nature, a U.S. Army veteran who served as a medic in Operation Desert Storm, with a warm laugh and unflappable optimism. She and her husband, who worked in sanitation at Hormel for most of his early career, decided to start their company one muggy night in the summer of 1996. As they sat around Alisa's kitchen table with her grandma and her husband's parents discussing her impending retirement from the military, they dreamed of a business they could eventually pass on to the next generation, something they could build all on their own. Alisa's mom later cautioned that getting a bank loan for the business would probably be tough, so they would have to finance it themselves.

Together, the family pooled their personal savings and used credit cards to buy the basics. They purchased mops, brooms, and other cleaning supplies. There were times when Alisa even brought her three young children along in the evenings to help empty trash, vacuum, and scrub toilets in the high-rise office buildings the firm serviced around Atlanta.

As the company landed larger new accounts, they eventually wanted to hire more cleaners. The Clarks decided to apply for a small-business loan, even after Alisa's mom and a volunteer assigned to them through the nonprofit Service Corps of Retired Executives (SCORE) discouraged them from even trying. Alisa and her husband still bristle when they recall their SCORE mentor, a curmudgeonly white gentleman, who quickly dismissed cleaning companies "like theirs" as "a dime a dozen" and assured them that they would be out of business in five years, and if not in five years, then ten. Apparently, it had been lost on this cynic that they had already been successfully operating for seven years. Undeterred, Alisa and her husband applied for a small loan from the bank they used for their checking and savings accounts. The bank had merged so many times by 2003 that she could barely remember its latest name and certainly did not have a close relationship with any of the loan officers.

They urgently needed to borrow money so they could accept a plum opportunity to clean a major Atlanta landmark managed by a government agency. It would take Glory to the next level. Alisa could barely sleep knowing her company couldn't do it unless it had enough cash to make payroll every two weeks for all the new help she would have to hire. But just as her mother predicted, the bank denied the loan and Glory Professional Cleaning had to walk away from the contract. Looking back, Alisa says there was no way Glory could have taken the account without an injection of capital to bridge the gap between paydays and when the prospective client would have settled its bill, most likely after thirty days or more. She couldn't make the numbers work.

Faster Payments Now

While we fought to keep Nourish alive, we dove deep into our project with John. In fact, as we evolved our brainstorming, we often swapped ideas about how to do what FTRANS and the marketplace figured could not be done. John decided to step away from FTRANS and became our cofounder in a brand-new venture.

As we talked about our mutual credit card inspiration, the three of us zeroed in on the fact that big customers prefer their suppliers' "free and flexible trade credit." They dictate the terms to their advantage. We recognized the disincentive to pay up sooner. For corporate America, it's baked into the business model. Same for government agencies that buy from small businesses. As we mentioned early in the book, small and medium-size business sellers of goods and services in the U.S. hold about $1.2 trillion in accounts receivable at any point in time. Over the course of a year, these businesses will give over $11 trillion to their business and government customers.

Taking on the System

We knew we couldn't just blow up the system. It seemed like the entire U.S. economy hinged on the free credit flowing to big companies. Our goal was to invent a payment solution that enabled both sides of the commerce transaction to get what they needed: the small supplier could get paid immediately without the cost and risk of loans or factoring, and the large commercial or government customer could get the free credit they were used to with accounts payable. This would enable small businesses to grow and would level the playing field.

Losing Nourish was a death of a thousand cuts and some mistakes, but largely we faced walls we couldn't scale and forces that we couldn't see until we were too deep inside the matrix of financing and cash flow. Once we uncovered the hidden weakness in the system—the slow pace of commerce hurting small businesses like ours—we saw an opportunity. The lesson here is that it's easy to feel powerless when you encounter failure caused by a systemic problem. Too often, the flaws feel personal, and entrepreneurs are hardwired to take the blame. *If only I hadn't* . . . becomes a mantra, and *I should have* . . . echoes in like a claxon. Yes, we'll make mistakes, but when the problem is in the system, you can't take the responsibility for not knowing before you could possibly know. Resist the self-flagellation and focus instead on what entrepreneurs do best. Once you identify a structural flaw, remind yourself that your discovery might actually be your biggest opportunity.

Our solution to speed up the cash-flow cycle for small companies really took shape one afternoon when John met with us in our tiny office in the fall of 2010. Collectively, the three of us had a 360-degree view of the problem. And that is rare. Typically, at most you have a 180-degree view of a problem. You either know the customer's side or the back-end execution side. John knew the back end of factoring and credit, and we knew the small-business-user side. Stacey, as COO, brought the real experience of balancing how you make sure that the difference between the money coming in and the money going out doesn't leave you in the lurch. Lara's customer-facing role was equally fraught as she pitched new accounts knowing they would surely ask for extended payment terms that would dig us deeper into debt.

Connect the Dots

Over three hours, we each took turns writing on a giant white flip pad. We jotted down everything that existed in the small-business lending ecosystem: SBA loans, bank loans, bank lines of credit, merchant cash advances, online lending, factoring, you name it. Then we broke down the pain points for small businesses, like personal guarantees, debt and liability on your balance sheet, hidden pricing in loans, and inflexible term contracts. We also considered what worked for the capital sources, and why lenders pushed such restrictions as collateral and demonstrable cash flow on small businesses in the first place: *What were they trying to manage or prevent?*

We looked at what was left over once the friction of loans and factoring were removed and compared our list to what we liked about the credit card. We were inspired. With credit cards, the merchant gets paid 100 percent of their actual revenue immediately, not an advance or a loan against their revenue. The merchant pays a service fee to the credit card company that does not change based on when and if the customer pays their Visa bill, so both sides get what they want. The merchant gets paid when and how they like (immediately), and the customer pays when and how they like (later).

There is no stigma attached to accepting a card for payment. Everyone wants to get paid faster. The credit card transaction does not add debt or liability to the balance sheet. The money the merchant gets is not owed back to anyone. The process is simple and there are no personal guarantees attached to the money.

Once we had all the pieces written on paper and laid out for us to see, we could dive deeper into each specific element and make connections. We began to look at the history of the credit card and how it became a game changer for consumers and retailers. Prior to the arrival of the credit card system, retailers were largely mom-and-pop stores. Many of them offered house accounts or tabs to customers as a way to build loyalty. If you shopped there you could purchase something, and instead of paying cash, you could put it on your charge account and pay the bill at the end of the month. In fact, collectively retailers funded more credit to consumers than financial institutions did. When the first all-purpose credit card, the BankAmericard, came out in 1958 from Bank of America, it was mainly small retailers that accepted it as a form of payment. The larger department stores had well-built-out credit departments. Lara remembers going with her mother every month to pay the Macy's bill, the Rich's bill, and the ThriftTown bill. The basement of Rich's and Macy's looked like a bank, with teller windows and dozens of clerks accepting checks for payment. After the bill was paid, she and her mom would shop. These large retailers didn't need to accept the bank credit card when they had their own, which they viewed as their competitive advantage. The little retailers gladly accepted the bank card as it enabled them to compete with their larger competitors. Over time, all retailers, large and small, realized it was more cost effective to accept Visa, Mastercard, and American Express than to run their own in-house credit. Today, most consumer credit is funded through the credit card system. Even large retailers with plenty of cash and access to cheap capital accept the credit card and pay a merchant fee for the service of getting paid immediately instead of funding their own in-house credit facilities, house accounts, or tabs. With a better understanding of the evolution of the credit card and our conclusions about the gaps in the lending ecosystem, we connected the dots. We thought we just might be on the edge of creating something equally transformative for business-to-business (B2B) as the credit card system had been for business-to-consumer (B2C).

Within months of collaborating with John, we developed the concept for a new kind of financial services company powered by technology, or fintech. We came up with the name NowAccount. When Lara suggested the name, John replied that a NowAccount was a "negotiable order of withdrawal" that the "old thrifts" used as checking accounts. We had never heard of such a thing as a Now-Account or a thrift. It turns out these outdated terms referred to relics of savings and loan institutions that had fallen by the wayside long before we were old enough to know what a bank was. The old trademarks had lapsed, and we successfully trademarked the words Now and NowAccount for financial services and online platforms.

We envisioned Now Corp being financed by the sale of bonds,

like the credit card industry. American Express sells bonds to banks and large funds, then uses the money from the sale of the bonds to pay the retailer when you use your card to buy something. This capital is much cheaper than borrowing money from a bank or using their own equity, but it can only be done in large amounts, so this type of structure is not available to small businesses. We wanted to develop a one-stop shop online platform that would enable businesses to convert outstanding IOUs almost immediately into not only cash, but actual revenue. Now would *not* be a factor. It would not be a lender. It would buy an unpaid invoice from a business and in exchange give that business the cash owed within days, minus a 3 percent flat fee. Now would assume the risk of nonpayment. The business would have received their actual revenue, and the fee would not change if the customer paid late or failed to pay, as long as the goods or service were delivered, just like the credit card system.

Now would vet its small-business clients as well as their customers in a streamlined way to assess how likely it was that the invoice would be paid, just the way a credit card company decides a transaction quickly when you swipe a card. But we knew we needed to better understand the risk built into our underwriting and test it with real transactions.

Luckily, Stacey discovered a federal program that would insure innovative loans to small businesses in each state. The short-term initiative under the State Small Business Credit Initiative (SSBCI) seemed like the natural partner for our pilot, so Stacey got on the phone to start researching it and see if we could find a way to get involved, and John got to work designing how the program would work for us.

Sticky Floor versus Glass Ceiling

Although we had John's expertise to rely on, fintech was a whole new domain for the two of us to master. But as we had with manufacturing water bottles, we approached it with the optimistic attitude that self-doubt was the only thing that could keep us from trying. Often people in marginalized groups focus on the glass ceiling they have to break through to succeed. But self-doubt is a sticky floor. Your own lack of confidence can hold you down, and you have to make sure you don't let your insecurities keep you from taking a leap. It's not easy. We had to be bold and admit what we didn't know. We turned that into our superpower by asking lots of questions and noticing things that bankers and people who had spent careers in financial services could only see through the lens of a loan. We were coming from the demand side of the problem, whereas the finance experts were looking at things from the supply side. We saw that "access to capital" did not have to be limited to lending, factoring, equity, or finance, but instead could be addressed by accelerated payments. We observed that small businesses are often talked "at" and not "with." They are told what they can and can't do by a banker who has never run a small business. They are told how and when they will get paid by large corporate and government customers. We noticed what a difference it would make if the solution to cash-flow problems came with predictable, simple, and flat pricing and without hidden fees. We realized that small businesses lend more than they ever borrow, because until an invoice is paid by the commercial customer, it's a free loan.

Many people think the word *pivot* means to change direction. But that's incomplete. To an engineer, the word refers to the central point on which a mechanism turns. You keep an anchor foot on the floor when you turn, and we did so without abandoning Nourish. The pivot we made to launch our new startup was rooted in our strong partnership and our quest to understand and fix our own cash-flow problems. We were able to seize this opportunity by keeping one foot anchored to our "why," and it turned into a whole new chapter for us as entrepreneurs. We pivoted into fintech but hoped our solution would help keep Nourish alive. With a team focused on this new opportunity, and with Brittany still helping us manage Nourish, NowAccount was born. Next, we had to track down financing and partners to put our new startup to the test.

LEVEL-UP LESSONS: CHAPTER 8

- It is easy to feel powerless when you experience failure but you must look at the root causes of the failure. If you failed, maybe others did too for the same reason. These are big opportunities!

- When tackling a problem, get a 360-degree view. Most people naturally have, at best, a 180-degree view. Find someone who sees the other side and include them in the development of the solution.

- Think outside the box and look outside your market for inspiration. Just as our inspiration for

NowAccount came from lunch at a restaurant and not at a fintech meeting, your greatest inspiration typically happens when you are not trying to solve a problem. Be open and curious.

- When solving a problem, use an engineering mindset. Describe the problem or points of friction in as much detail as you can before you start to design a solution that connects all the dots.

- Sometimes what is holding you back is not a glass ceiling but rather a sticky floor. Don't let your self-doubt overcome you. Why shouldn't *you* be the one to solve this problem?

- The key to a successful pivot is the pivot foot, your anchor. Without an anchor, you are changing direction and wandering. Be intentional about what cannot change no matter what direction you are facing. Is it your customer, your mission, your product?

9

KNOW YOUR NUMBERS

The year 2011 began with a number of new ventures. Now had moved to center stage for us and John, and the concept was deceptively simple: purchase the invoices of small businesses who couldn't afford to wait to get paid by other businesses. Of course, if it was easy, someone would have done it before. We huddled together at all hours of the day, sifting through research, testing models, and identifying pain points. Lara led ideation sessions where we riffed on the different approaches we could take, and John poked holes into previous solutions that had failed to address the core issues crippling companies like Nourish and others. Stacey read through reams of analysis on financial regulations and policy solutions that had never quite done the job.

In addition to the soft launch of Now, Stacey had her own change of direction. The previous November, her Democratic colleagues in the House had elected her to serve as minority leader. The promotion even came with a new perch. She moved up to the front of the House Chamber, across the aisle from her Republican counterpart, the majority leader. Both of them sat directly in front of the dais from which the Speaker of the House convened the chamber each day of the legislative session. Before, when her day job beckoned, Stacey could discreetly slip from her desk into the anteroom and sneak into one of the antique wooden phone booths to take a call. Her new role denied her such discretion, but she had to make it work.

Get a Life

Being the successful multihyphenate she is, Stacey has always been skilled at intently tuning in to one thing at a time no matter how many things she has going on. Whether penning novels, calculating spreadsheets, or debating bills in committee, she prioritizes being present and directing her undivided attention with precision. But she also understands the obligation to shift gears from one mode to the next.

One of the traits we share and appreciate in each other is the way we optimize our time. We used to joke that we could have made a lot more money when we had Insomnia Consulting if we hadn't optimized our time so much. If we had only billed clients for the hours it would take most people to do the same work, we could have really cashed in.

It comes down to our acceptance of a truth—"work-life balance" is a myth. If your life is completely in balance (and whose is?), it's like a seesaw standing still, your feet just dangling, going nowhere— and that's no fun. It also means everything's just average. Lara has no desire to be an average mom, an average wife, or an average CEO, and Stacey has no desire to be an average leader, an average businessperson, or an average daughter, sister, or aunt. While we do agree entrepreneurship requires focus and dedication, we have never believed that owning a business should come at the expense of having a life.

With Stacey's responsibilities at the Capitol heating up, we approached this new phase of our partnership and personal goals with the same discipline and efficiency we always did. We had a frank discussion about how her expertise served the new company. At Now, Stacey took on the role of senior vice president and continued her work behind the scenes managing operations and providing general legal counsel. Lara rightly stepped into the public-facing role she flourished in as president and CEO, with the responsibility to guide our capital raise and structure this disruptive concept into a profitable company. John served as chairman and chief credit officer, and he brought his deep experience from FTRANS and an avid curiosity about how to tackle this new challenge. We rounded out our initial team with staff from John's previous gigs and ours, including contractors who could help us go to market swiftly and intelligently. Because Now was a fintech, we had to address both the service we offered—monetizing invoices—and the delivery mechanism—a seamless interaction that minimized paperwork and was as automated as possible. One of the appeals of the credit card has always been the ease of use. Now not only had to feel the same, it had to operate the same way. Otherwise, potential customers might see us as yet another hassle rather than a solution.

We initially funded startup costs ourselves, along with investments from former business colleagues who understood cash-flow issues, and some early clients who wanted in. Because we were closer to the tech space than to manufacturing, fundraising came much more easily. Now raised $2.5 million by 2013 to cover the development of the platform and to pay the first employees to run it. Our next capital source, which we used to accelerate payments to our clients, was several credit unions. We took out lines of credit with Amplify Credit Union in Texas, and Peach State and MembersFirst Credit Unions in Georgia. These were small lines totaling $3 million, and we had an additional subordinated line of $1.7 million from a credit union service organization for a total of almost $5 million in capital. Each dollar of debt we had could accelerate about seven dollars of invoices in a year, because we could accelerate a dollar and then the invoice would get paid fifty days later, and we could accelerate another dollar, and do this seven times a year. We were on our way.

Split Shifts

By this point in our journey, we had found a rhythm that worked for the two of us, even if it was unconventional; but we needed to communicate the dynamic to the rest of our team. To maintain cohesion and trust, leaders must keep defining and redefining everyone's roles her role in the company, and she laid out clear guidelines about never representing the company before the state in any fashion. They would have lots to fight about in the coming years, but Now would not be a point of contention.

Front and Back of the House

We faced competing schedules and a growing staff, but we never forgot our respective roles. Sometimes, though, we had to remind staff and gently redirect questions or concerns when an eager team member sought to circumvent the system to get a favorable response. Both of us had managed large staffs before, but for the first time we were managing more than four people—not including ourselves—together. That meant we had to be extra careful about how we served their needs and grew our capacity. Rule one was that we never undermined each other by taking on the other's responsibilities. Lara set company policy and Stacey handled HR, not vice versa. When the two came into conflict, we would discuss the issues and find the best practice. As information flew around the office, we went out of our way to avoid stepping on each other's toes. Even when we disagreed, we never did so in public or in front of staff. Startups feel incredibly fragile, and the Sturm und Drang of office politics is the quickest way to heighten staff anxiety. We did our best to always maintain a unified front, though we debated in our typical "Yes . . . but" fashion out of staff view. Our offline discussions could be intense; we are the type of people who need *all*

as the company grows. More importantly, being explicit about responsibilities is an imperative, even if your team doesn't work split shifts like ours. In a startup, everyone is wearing lots of hats, but as you scale, clarity avoids misunderstanding and mistakes.

Scaling also demands that those in charge learn to delegate, and when appropriate, to let go of certain tasks. This sounds simple, but entrepreneurs—especially those on a second or third go—worry that if you don't keep your hand in everything, you'll miss something. Unfortunately, what may be intended as protectiveness comes across as defensive or, worse, as rank arrogance that makes others wonder why they should stick around. An important corollary to letting go is that no one should be wedded to a particular title or a specific role, because evolution is inevitable in an early-stage company. At Now, Lara was president, but her role soon included liaison to credit unions and community banks. Stacey began as SVP, but soon her office in the back of Nourish's old haunts became HR. John started as chairman, but he became our default CTO as we started to grow our tech. When we needed fresh eyes or new ideas, each of us had to make room for those better suited to the task.

As Now picked up momentum, we saw how essential it was to our overall company culture and the health of our nascent venture that every team member we brought on understood the structure of our organization and that it was evolving. Whether that meant Lara's crisscrossing the country because investors required constant reassurance, or Stacey's late-night communiqués about payroll, adaptation and flexibility were more than skills—they were core values of Now.

Stacey in particular worked the graveyard shift, putting her time into the operations of the business late at night, as she had at Insomnia and Nourish. This is when she worked through the underwriting, which included consulting with the U.S. Treasury Department, to integrate SSBCI and its insurance program for lenders into Now's pilot. She drafted legal documents and correspondence, worked with John to understand the various state SSBCI programs outside of Georgia and how they might fit our model, and built the HR and administrative infrastructure. Most important to the growth of Now, even in the middle of the night she wrote emails that teed up important meetings with prospective partners where Lara could pitch Now when the sun came up. Our team had to understand that even if Stacey couldn't put in facetime in the office from January to March because she was at the Capitol, she was still essential to the operation. If she couldn't respond to something during business hours, staff came to expect an email from her in their in-box first thing next morning. While we were accustomed to this working dynamic, it was new for John and the other team members, so we had to constantly revisit roles and adjust as needed.

One afternoon, Stacey joined us at a senior staff meeting in the conference room of our offices. The annual legislative session had ended. But in August, she would be called back into a special session for redistricting, when the legislative lines for all congressional, state house, and state senate seats would be adopted for the next ten years. John had once interned for the venerable U.S. senator Sam Nunn, and he approved of Stacey's time in the legislature. However, Now was reaching a critical point in development, and his modus operandi called for all hands on deck—and in the office. We had

worked around these issues before, but Stacey could sense hi comfort with her upcoming schedule, and she understood ho it seemed that she would be away from their company home a a key inflection point. Rather than let the tension hover ov conversation, Stacey called it out and invited conversation. Lar the consummate leader, encouraged questions from John and teammates. She chimed in with supportive statements abou cey's work habits but she also exhorted folks to lift up conc real time. Allowing worry to fester in such a small group cou lead to chaos, and our mutual respect gave us the space to w pushback and the confidence to accept it. Though these would flare again from time to time, we all understood tha lems only get solved when they are exposed.

We not only had to optimize Stacey's time, but also c clear demarcation between her political work and Now Cor was especially important given the hotly partisan climate state. Until her campaign for minority leader, the partnersh Lara, a Republican political appointee, hadn't attracted m tention or scrutiny. But Stacey's opponents didn't hesitate t to question her loyalties once she won the post. When sl umphed in a contentious bid to lead House Democrats, l order of business as minority leader was to debate prioritie newly elected GOP governor, including the fate of a belo lege scholarship program and a tight budget. Part of Nov ness model included participation in a federal program, an knew that although the law permitted the company's partic the optics also mattered. She went to visit the attorney g Republican, and to see the governor's team. Both were inf

the information to make a decision. But while we took the work seriously, we did not consider ourselves to be infallible. We also tend to defer to the other's expertise. And after we had our off-camera debates, we presented a united front with whatever resolution we decided on.

We both think on our feet and know that it's hard to win an argument when you're fighting someone who thinks as quickly as you do. There's no imbalance in our partnership. And so, to win, you've got to really win. When we would disagree on something, the level playing field of respect made us instantly realize that we were both looking at the same question differently. In Now's early days, we had to decide where to invest our limited capital. One of us favored marketing in order to tell our story, but the other preferred tech improvements to speed our delivery to customers. These choices struck us as fundamental, and so we debated every angle. Tech improvements won out (no, we won't say whose idea it was). Marketing got delayed but not diminished. Instead, because of the discussion, we found a lower-cost option for marketing that evolved into one of our signature programs. Although the outcome satisfied us both in the long run, we had each dug in and wanted to win. But we always return to respect. Even today when we don't see eye to eye, this dynamic creates intrigue and curiosity, impelling both of us to step back and ask, "What am I missing?" The enduring thing that always allowed hard conversations to happen between us was that neither of us ever wanted to quit. We never entered a debate in which the solution was *not* to act. We always found a way forward.

Hello! Small Business

We had figured out the big systemic problem we wanted to solve for small businesses and developed a working business model and how to finance the first stages of it. Now we needed to focus on persuading entrepreneurs that they needed NowAccount. Because we were building an entirely new infrastructure for a new financial product, we needed an efficient way to reach small businesses in every corner of the economy, as well as a marketing pitch that was easy to grasp. One of the most difficult hurdles, both for Now and for small businesses across the U.S., is that small-business owners operate mainly in isolation. They are completely disaggregated. It's hard to reach owners on a mass scale because they don't generally interact unless they are doing business directly with each other. As Lara likes to say, small-business owners hide in plain sight. If you walked into a restaurant at noon and looked around, you would have no idea who in the room owned a business. They typically don't sit around wearing T-shirts with logos or meet in one central cafeteria or club on a given day. The fragmented landscape meant that for us to spread the word about NowAccount, we would need to enlist the help of parties that already had a trusted voice with small businesses. But it didn't make sense to hire a big sales team or spend tons of money on billboards and ads just yet. Instead, we needed to be strategic about how to leverage our network. We learned that if your customers are hard to reach, figure out who they listen to for advice and leverage those voices as a way to introduce your product or service.

The Flow of Commerce

From our experience with Nourish and our crushing defeat, we knew that we had to think carefully about what we could promise our new clients and what we could deliver. One of the biggest mistakes entrepreneurs often make is overpromising to a customer before the product is solid or they have the operations and suppliers in place to keep up with their obligations, leading to underdelivering. Remember, sustainable commerce is a *flow, not an event*. Closing one sale does not mean you have sustainable commerce. You have to retain the customer through excellent delivery and service. If you are not ready to do that, then you don't want that customer. While the first sale is exciting, you have to always be thinking about the tenth sale and beyond.

We had to figure out a robust link to small businesses that we could manage while we were still small. Through her political network, Stacey had strong connections to many of the people around Georgia who advocated for minority-owned businesses. She laid the groundwork for valuable meetings with the Georgia Minority Supplier Development Council, the Hispanic Chamber of Commerce, and the Georgia Credit Union Affiliates. John's chance meeting with a credit union executive at a wedding combined with Stacey's relationship with their state leaders led to a deep relationship with credit unions that has been a part of every phase of Now's growth and evolution. Along with the Georgia Chamber of Commerce, credit unions would become our first partners and enable Lara to make inroads with trusted institutions that could pull together dozens of small businesses in a single meeting. Chambers and membership organizations would offer NowAccount to their members at a discount and we would be able to receive customer feedback quickly.

When the team met with the head of Georgia's Credit Union League, Mike Mercer, who, coincidentally, had also chaired the Credit Union National Association, the lobbying arm of the credit union industry, his interest was piqued. He told us that while many credit unions were not set up to do small-business lending, they were very interested in helping fill the void in the small-business space left by retreating banks, just as credit unions had played a similar role and stepped up to serve consumers decades ago when banks did not. He had been hearing from other credit unions across the country that members were eager for help getting access to capital for their small businesses because there were no longer many avenues to securing loans from community banks. He thought Now-Account might be a turnkey solution. The credit union leagues of Georgia, Texas, California, Ohio, and Iowa eventually signed on as our first partners. And as we planned, the SSBCI program helped us stress-test the way we funded the business and made NowAccount available to more small businesses. And it decreased the risk we took on, as the Treasury Department guaranteed funds if a client went out of business and could not deliver their goods or service.

What's a Bip?

We learned very quickly that establishing trust, even if it was uncomfortable, was the key to building our client base. In our early conversations with small-business owners, they were downright skeptical of NowAccount, asking us, "What's the catch?" or "Is this just factoring?" We knew many small-business owners were already frustrated by the current financial environment, and many had been burned by predatory lenders or been squeezed out of the market as credit dried up during and after the financial crisis. They were tired, distrustful of the system, and used to being dictated to by banks and their big customers.

This could not have been more evident on a Wednesday morning at Georgia State University as Lara took the stage at the Small Business Finance Institute's "Stepping Up to Business" Conference, where she was slated to discuss "Thinking Outside the Bank." It was one of the first times she would talk about NowAccount in public. Up to this point, our startup had been flying under the radar, so this was a chance to float the concept with Now's target market of small and midsize B2B business owners. As the seats began to fill up, Lara was filled with nervous energy and excitement as she took note of the wide-eyed enthusiasm of the crowd.

In her colorful shift dress and trademark statement necklace, Lara stood out next to the other three white male panelists in their formal, dark suits. She was slated to introduce herself after the men on the panel as she was seated furthest from the moderator. As she waited patiently while each one took a turn throwing around intimidating and confusing finance lingo, she watched the audience members' energy deflate. They slumped lower and lower in their seats with each successive panelist's spiel about the challenges of obtaining capital. Speakers threw around terms like "bips" (aka basis points); the "Five Cs of Credit"; factoring; equity; guarantees;

and dilution, without taking the time to explain anything in plain English.

Lara expertly read the room. This was just another instance when small-business owners were being talked down to. By the time she was up, she was ready to turn the tables.

She smiled and in her friendly Southern drawl asked for a show of hands.

"First of all, who knows what a 'bip' is, and how many of you think it is something bad on your computer screen that you just want to go away?"

The whole room burst out laughing. With her wit, she acknowledged that no one understood all the jargon the other speakers had just arrogantly thrown at them. And then she began to speak, business owner to business owner. The mood lifted immediately.

"How many of you sell a product? How many of you sell a service?" she inquired. Hands went up, heads nodded, and suddenly she was having a conversation with them that felt meaningful. It felt good. Lara went on to share all the ups and downs of Nourish. It was a major aha moment. NowAccount could stand out by meeting people where they were. Lara spoke their language and conveyed that we knew exactly what they were going through. In the world of finance and fintech, NowAccount could be different simply by being authentic and acknowledging straight up that all of this is intimidating. And that it's even more confusing when you don't fully grasp how money works in your business.

Know Your Numbers

We have never known anyone who started a business because they have a passion for finance and accounting. Lenders, suppliers, customers, and anyone you do business with might throw around fancy terms, assuming that you're familiar with them. The reality is that most people are not, and probably don't fully understand their balance sheets either. Most people don't like to admit that they are intimidated by financial lingo. Instead of taking the time to understand the difference between assets and liabilities, they run the other way or ignore their lack of understanding until they are in deep trouble. But *knowing your numbers is a necessary evil for your business to stay in business.* The biggest thing you can do for your company is to bite the bullet and try to break down your business finances into the simplest terms.

Bankers use a lot of gobbledygook that makes it sound scary, but that's just job preservation for them. It's to their advantage to make it all sound so complicated. Understanding your business isn't that hard when you get the accountingspeak out of the way and just say to yourself, *"Where does my money go every day and where does my money come from every day? And at what cadence does it come in versus out?"* If you understand that, then you really understand the financials of your business, and you can be empowered to make the best choices at the right time. It can be as simple as taking out a sheet of white paper and drawing every connection that your business has to other parties— your ecosystem. This includes customers, suppliers, partners, and investors. Then, look at each one and at the form, flow, and timing of money back and forth. When you do this often, you find that capital can come in many forms and in the most unlikely of places.

Yes, there are structural problems with the way financial institutions deal with small-business owners, but small-business owners also need to take ownership of their finances. Lack of financial literacy is one of the most impactful hidden forces hobbling small-business owners. Some researchers who study entrepreneurship call for a new high school graduation requirement in U.S. public schools that includes a basic understanding of finance.

"Financial literacy among entrepreneurs and would-be entrepreneurs is a major issue for two basic reasons. First, lots of research has demonstrated that Americans in general are woefully ignorant about even the basics of finance," John Dearie of the Center for American Entrepreneurship told us. "And second, understanding the capital needs of one's startup—what do I really need?—and knowing how to raise sufficient capital at reasonable terms are vitally important skills for entrepreneurs. Put those two realities together and you have the makings of a major obstacle to successful entrepreneurship."

The important thing to remember is that if you feel overwhelmed by numbers you are not alone. But rather than suffer in silence, you must seek out support from other business owners and opportunities to access coaching. The help you need is not from a banker who has never run a business. It's from someone who has been in the trenches and knows exactly what it feels like to stay awake at night worrying about keeping the lights on. Small Business Development Centers and SCORE webinars can offer free help. Networking groups in your particular industry can be also invaluable. And of course, hiring professionals to handle your finances as you grow is essential, as well as reevaluating their skills level along the way. A bookkeeper and an accountant may be fine in the startup phase, but as your business scales and becomes more complex, you may need to upgrade to a CFO and a more sophisticated CPA. Even if you invest in professional help, *you* still need to comprehend how money moves in and out of your business. When you hire experts, make sure they speak in lay terms, not in jargon, and be assertive in pushing them to translate so you don't get lost. Don't fall into the trap of being embarrassed by terms you don't understand. You hired experts to make it clear. Ask for a coaching session to teach you how to read basic financials and a cheat sheet on which metrics matter most. And if you have difficulty reading financials, try drawing a graphic representation on paper. The bottom line is that ignoring your finances comes at your peril. If you don't take the initiative to take a hard look at your numbers, you can never level up.

We also found that businesses that either supply or purchase from you can be a source of information, advice, and even capital. When Scott Curlee of Inmark offered to cover the fifty thousand dollars for the Nourish molds and amortize the costs over time, it was an out-of-the-box solution we hadn't even considered. Sometimes owning the fact that you don't know everything and being willing to ask questions can lead you to transformative answers.

One of the questions we had to ask ourselves as we continued to expand NowAccount was where we could find clients in the most efficient and impactful manner. The answer might surprise you. Our whole mission was to help small-business owners rewire how quickly they got paid from big corporations and government agencies. We knew the power imbalance was deeply embedded and not likely to change anytime soon. But what if big business could help the little guy in a counterintuitive way? We figured it might be worth a try.

LEVEL-UP LESSONS: CHAPTER 9

- Entrepreneurs have lives too. You do not have to give up your personal life to be an entrepreneur. This is a fallacy propagated by those who have sacrificed their personal lives and want company.

- Roles evolve. Don't get married to your title.

- To secure your first customers, look at who your ideal customers trust and partner with them to leverage their voice.

- Get advice from people who have been in your shoes, not people who have read about shoes. Has your banker ever run a small business? When they give you advice, ask to speak with another small-business owner they have helped.

- Know your numbers and the story behind your balance sheet. You don't need to have studied accounting or finance, but make sure that your bookkeeper, accountant, or CFO can clearly explain your numbers to you.

10

THE BIG BAD WOLF

The silhouette of Coca-Cola's corporate headquarters looms over our hometown. The iconic curvy-red logo shines across the top of the granite edifice, cheerily familiar. But it's a whole different story on the ground below, Lara thought, as she drove up to the fortresslike compound in the fall of 2014. She was on her way to meet with the global beverage giant's chief procurement officer to learn more about the company's supply chain, especially how it worked with small and diverse businesses. Behind imposing door after imposing door, and after multiple security screenings, Lara was directed to a visitor waiting room (stocked with plenty of beverages, of course) with only a few other fidgeting, hopeful vendors, eager for their host to come and escort them. The whole experience was intimidating, exactly the way many small-business owners feel when they interact with the mega companies they regard as their dream customers. Even Lara, whose husband, Casey, had arranged this meeting and had worked for Coke for two decades, still couldn't help but feel like Dorothy waiting to meet the Wizard.

The irony was that she was sitting there at all, hoping to partner with Coke. When we conceived of NowAccount, we sought to help small businesses level the playing field when working with Goliaths like Coke. We had been burned by the financial system that privileged the big B in B2B transactions, and we hadn't forgotten the pain. But as we studied the power imbalance between large companies and the small firms that make up their supply chains, we began to understand that although it might seem as if corporate America operated like the Big Bad Wolf, the intent wasn't necessarily nefarious. Small firms were the collateral damage in the increasingly fast-paced, tech-powered battle for profitability and Wall Street dominance.

Inside the Emerald City

We realized that huge multinational conglomerates are the largest aggregator of small businesses. Many of them attempt to help small businesses through supplier diversity programs. But it is often a Catch-22 for everyone involved. The corporate giants say they want to buy more from underrepresented and diverse businesses, but their common practices, like taking months to negotiate a contract and taking even longer to pay invoices, threaten the survival of those very companies. This is a routine point of tension between procurement officers, who manage relationships with vendors and try to maintain a strong and sustainable supply chain of products and services, and CFOs, who often delay payments and stretch out their payables (which is the only free capital they have) to optimize their cash flow and shore up the bottom line. In so doing, they risk putting small vendors out of business. It is an inherent tug-of-war. And when the CFOs win out, as they usually do, and a small business suffers under the weight of the terms and can't deliver, the problem reverts to the procurement officer, who is forced to find another vendor to take the job. The whole situation is frustrating, costly, and reinforces the misperception that small businesses are too risky and unable to deliver.

In Coke's case, we learned that there were tens of thousands of supplier businesses providing goods and services to the company. That's way more than any local Chamber of Commerce or credit union, our existing partners, has in membership. We theorized that if we explained how Now could help corporations assist their supplier businesses, perhaps Coke and other multibillion-dollar companies would become the gateway for NowAccount to reach even more clients. We also knew that there is nobody a small-business owner listens to more than its prized customers, so hearing about NowAccount from Coke could be a game changer for us. We had nothing to lose.

Coke's procurement chief, Ron Lewis, introduced Lara to the vice president of Global Supplier Diversity, a firebrand named Terrez Thompson, who had spent her life pushing the envelope to look for opportunities to support people of color, women, and anyone she felt was underserved or not being treated fairly. Born and raised in Baltimore by a single mother, Terrez was a Coke veteran known around the office as a straight shooter. She had seen it all and didn't mask her skepticism before she had even heard a word of Lara's pitch. In fact, she later admitted to Lara that the only reason she took the meeting was because her boss told her she had to. People were always trying to hawk predatory proposals dressed up as "solutions" to help disadvantaged businesses, and Terrez was convinced that few financial instruments really helped them. She wasn't inclined to touch NowAccount with a ten-foot pole.

But she did listen to what Lara had to say. By the end of their chat, she couldn't deny she'd found Lara's energy infectious. What struck her was the way Lara talked from her own deeply personal experiences about the pain points facing small-business owners. Terrez decided to give Now and Lara a shot. There was a minority "vendor day" coming up, when hundreds of small firms would gather at Coke to tour and learn all about opportunities to do business with the company, as well as a Mentor Protégé class sponsored by the Georgia Minority Supplier Development Council that would be held at the Coca-Cola facility. Lara would be given a speaking slot at both events. But Terrez cut to the chase, and in her typical no-nonsense style she told Lara she probably wouldn't stick around to hear Lara's presentation.

Lara wasn't deterred by Terrez's candor and looked ahead to both events with excitement. On the day of the Mentor Protégé class, Coke's cavernous auditorium on the main floor buzzed with anticipation. There was a shared sense of wonder at being inside the Coke "castle" among the hundreds of entrepreneurs who felt lucky to have been invited. Each dreamed of landing a contract with the beverage behemoth. As promised, Terrez hastily introduced Lara and planned to slip out quickly. But as Lara shared the story of how she and Stacey had built and lost Nourish, the audience leaned in, and Terrez decided to stick around. She saw them listening intently to the anguish in Lara's voice as she revealed how Nourish had grown out of business, some of them nodding along. Soon Lara's talk began to build to an emotional crescendo. And as she laid out the premise behind NowAccount, that small firms serve as "indentured lenders" to their big clients and that her company was trying to rewrite the rules to get them paid faster, the room erupted in whoops and cheers.

A woman stood up and called out, "Yeah, why are *we* the free bank?"

"This is amazing!" another man shouted as he rose to his feet.

Soon everyone was standing and applauding. What had started out as a staid corporate workshop had quickly turned into something resembling a Baptist revival. Lara looked over and saw Terrez grinning in the doorway, just as taken aback by the effusive response as Lara.

The electric moment sparked a friendship with Terrez and a fruitful partnership with the Coca-Cola Company. Being on the inside of a large corporation and getting to know the businesses working with Coke afforded us a rare and an even closer look at how small and big work together.

Get Through the Nos

Terrez reinforced the lesson we had learned at Nourish: although working with a heavyweight can come with lots of rewards, it also comes with lots of unforeseen risks. We know it is not easy to get in the door when you are starting out or beginning to scale. Submitting a proposal through a supplier portal at a corporate giant or government agency can entail hundreds of hours of work. Terrez often tells entrepreneurs who aspire to work with large clients that they should assume it will take six months to a year or more to land a deal, and to build that time line into their business plan. Their revenue strategy should not depend on the big account until it's actually signed, sealed, and delivered—and the check is in their account.

One of the reasons it takes so long is that there is often no single person in a major organization who will offer the final and definitive yes. It's more about getting through all of the people who can say no. This is key to how you plot your strategy. It will take time to find your champions inside the target company. But remember that every person you meet, every touchpoint, could be a potential advocate or a potential no. This is especially important to remember when you get in the door via a relationship with a senior executive. All too often entrepreneurs falsely think that because the CEO or a senior executive walks them into the company, their deal is a done deal. You will have to build in time to hunt down and impress many stakeholders along the way, even after you've gotten your foot in the door and even when the person who brought you in is the

CEO. This is how contractor Jonathan Ford always approaches any project his firm is bidding on.

"I go into most scenarios, most companies, most organizations... I'm looking for my cheerleader. Who's my cheerleader? Who is the point person that people are listening to that I can talk to?" says Jonathan. "It doesn't have to be the CEO or CFO or whoever the case may be. It can be that office administrator that people run everything through, and she knows what's going on. It can be anybody; everybody has a value. You just have to figure out what that value is."

Remember, there's a long road ahead even after you get the green light. Terrez helped us understand the extent to which entrepreneurs don't fully comprehend the pressures on a small firm's operations when they try to do business with very large clients. One of the most common challenges is that the systems, policies, and paperwork are often one size fits all, whether you are a solo graphic designer, a fifty-person catering operation, or a two-hundred-person trucking company. This is a pervasive problem across all facets of the small-business landscape. Whether it's access to commerce or capital, the existing structures are not sized to account for the youth or the size of a business. After all, small businesses are not mini Fortune 100 companies, nor are their owners Fortune 100 CEOs. Yet they are expected to have the resources and the knowledge to function like much more established enterprises. Unfortunately, this is the way it is—for now—but going into these situations with your eyes open and prepared for a slog through bureaucracy can mean the difference between failure and your success.

Help Me Help You

For this reason, Terrez, who retired from Coke in 2020 after thirty-five years and founded a nonprofit to support Black and underserved entrepreneurs, cautions all suppliers to do their homework before pitching a major customer. You need to go in with open eyes about the requirements and expectations. In her straightforward manner, she says being a small business working with a giant customer can be a bit like being a mistress. In other words, don't ever fool yourself about where the loyalty lies in the end. In the fast-moving, post-COVID digital age, you must show that what you bring is new or different and will help the customer beat the competition.

Bring a solution, not a product. As Terrez says, "If you can come up with a solution for how to make them quicker, more nimble, more competitive, there are very few corporations, buyers, or business-people who won't listen, because it's that competitive." Focus on the impact of your product or service and not the product or service itself. You're selling ease, a competitive edge, or cost-savings—not a widget.

One way to demonstrate your impact is to solve a problem the customer doesn't even know they have. This is how our friend Traci Morgan elevated the reputation of her food and beverage engineering firm when she began work on a new contract with one of the largest industrial bakeries in Georgia. The snack-food maker had hired Morgan Consultants to help it expand the capacity of an existing plant, where it produced truckloads of cookies and crackers.

To give you a sense of scale, Traci works on projects that require five hundred to a thousand times the amount of flour or baking soda or salt used in a regular home kitchen. She was initially brought in to help with the conceptual design and preliminary engineering, and would advise on upgrades to equipment and controls. But when she visited the facility for the first time, she spotted some major safety flaws, including a risk for combustion and some sanitation problems, that she determined were either being missed, ignored, or swept under the rug.

Fixing safety and sanitation issues was not what she was hired to do, but she felt an obligation to raise her concerns with the client. Initially, her findings fell on deaf ears. She was frustrated but still took on the project and worked to make sure the hazards were properly documented. Traci even hired a mock auditor, with the client's blessing, to catalog all she had uncovered so that she could confirm there was a dangerous risk of explosion if action wasn't taken. In going the extra mile and not giving up, Traci proved her firm to be indispensable. The result? She eventually won multiple high-profile multimillion-dollar contracts with the same company to consult on plant expansions and modernization. Through her enterprise and persistence, she showed how her small firm could work quickly to save the client headaches, time, and money.

Look Under the Hood

Terrez encourages small firms to study the supply-chain businesses that already work with a big customer. She says this is an overlooked but incredibly effective way to land work indirectly with a Fortune 500 type of client. For example, most major corporations employ one or more larger established marketing agencies to help with creative concepts, but within the scope of work there may be multiple projects that require the lead agencies to hire smaller operators. Maybe they need graphic design help or a team of photographers or copywriting expertise? The umbrella agencies can be a valuable conduit of work for your small firm while shielding your business from the headaches of delayed payments or other capital-intensive aspects of the contract your business may not be ready to handle yet. But by looking under the hood at opportunities that feed into a big account, you get a proving ground and a chance to work with your dream customer in a way that is more insulated from financial risk. It also provides a chance to develop relationships with the bigger client, even if indirectly. And we can never reiterate enough that your network is your net worth.

Making the time to cultivate contacts so you can understand the businesses and competitors in your space is critical to eventually landing the major account. Sometimes, you can even team up with your competitors to pursue a big customer. Chambers of Commerce, local SBA offices, Minority Business Development Agency Centers, and national supplier diversity organizations are all networks you can join locally. You can also apply for certification of your business as a disadvantaged enterprise through the SBA and organizations like the National Minority Supplier Development Council or the National Association of Women Business Owners, which will give you entrée to exclusive networks that will help you build valuable connections and gain access to contracts set aside specifically for certified businesses. We know it takes work, but you have to think of it as an investment and build a strategy around understanding the ecosystem of large, medium, and small businesses that can be potential clients.

Power Play

One of the pitfalls we experienced with Nourish that is especially common in the world of consumer goods is the power dynamic between your small company and the retail marketplaces where you want to sell your products. Starting out, who doesn't want a deal with Target or Walmart? As we told you, even the two of us, a Yale-trained tax attorney and a Harvard MBA, still had trouble deciphering the implications of terms and conditions in our Nourish agreement with Whole Foods. But if you get the opportunity to go big, it is essential that you understand the forces at play.

Our friend Eva Jane Bunkley spent years rising before dawn to powder the noses of some of the world's biggest stars as they stopped by her makeup chair before an interview on *Good Day Atlanta*—everyone from Cicely Tyson to Jamie Foxx to The Rock to Usher. Eva Jane's Emmy Award–winning talent for making beautiful people look even more gorgeous on television earned her a fun living with tons of great stories. But after more than a decade, she wanted more flexibility to care for her two young boys. She had always been creative, and she'd started playing around with an idea for a new kind of sponge to apply foundation with the swipe of a finger.

"I vetted so many different materials because it needed to have a certain texture, a certain feel, a certain workability, pliability, malleability. It had an open-pore structure so that when you pick up that product, it'll deposit [the foundation] where you want it without having to dampen the sponge. It's meant to be used dry," she explained of her product's differentiating factor.

Once she found the right materials, she made a few samples, and they attracted notice from other makeup pros who saw her unique sponges in action. With their encouragement, she decided to go for it and start selling them. She cashed out thirty thousand dollars from her retirement account to patent and trademark her invention, buy the supplies, and line up a factory to manufacture the first run of sponges. Her signature product, the Makeup Bullet, was born.

The product became an overnight sensation at a European wholesale beauty supply trade show, and soon Eva Jane had distribution in shops all over Italy, Spain, the UK, Russia, South Africa, and Saudi Arabia. When she was invited to start selling it on a major international beauty website, she had to pinch herself. Eva Jane couldn't believe how quickly she hit the big time. A year later, she discovered that her dream customer was now selling a cheaper knock-off in its brick-and-mortar stores. She was livid and decided to make her own less-expensive version and began to sell it wholesale to other retailers in order to undercut the competition. But the huge retailer had more resources than her solo enterprise, and she couldn't compete.

Later, the Makeup Bullet was spotted by a buyer for a major department-store chain. Eva Jane jumped at the opportunity when she was promised a prime display on the retail floor in dozens of stores. But within weeks of signing the contract, she was told that the buyer didn't like the packaging for the Makeup Bullet and demanded that she design new boxes with a completely different look. She complied at her own expense. Eva Jane didn't think she had a choice and didn't want to jeopardize what seemed like a once-in-a-lifetime chance. But when the packaging was finished, she learned the retailer had also brought in a direct competitor to her product and gave their items a much more visible spot on the floor. When her products didn't sell well, she ended up stuck with lots of unsold inventory in packaging she loathed. Eventually, she went back to selling the Makeup Bullet and a few other of her beauty inventions directly through her website and social media. Being able to stay in control of the brand and to manage sales and marketing on her own without having to kowtow to demands was a relief, and she says she is much happier. One of the most important lessons Eva Jane says she learned is that entrepreneurs need to seek out advice from one another and to share their authentic experiences of dealing with large corporations. It's difficult to understand what you are really getting into unless you can talk to someone who has been through it. As she learned, small businesses don't often get a chance to control the competition, the product placement, or the marketing. But knowledge is power, and the more small businesses can be open about the ups and downs they encounter, the more information everyone has to go into these deals with eyes wide open.

Deal or No Deal

Getting bigfooted or feeling bullied by the gatekeepers is common. A new entrepreneur has no line of sight into other deals or even into what is fair. You could end up negotiating against yourself and not even realize what's happening until it's too late.

But there are ways to strengthen your position that don't require an MBA. One of the easiest ways to gain an advantage in a negotiation is to be quiet and let the other party talk. Sounds simple, but keeping your mouth shut can be hard to do when you want to impress the other side. We're often taught to jump right out there, anchor our position, and tell the decision maker what we want first. However, not being the first one to speak allows you to get a true sense of the state of play. Often, the other party will reveal some of their thinking about your business and why they took the meeting. Listen for cues about their concerns and what sparked their interest. When it is your time to talk, instead of peppering them with selling points about your business, try asking, "What would you like to accomplish?" Centering the conversation around how you can help their bottom line can be far more valuable than extolling your own virtues. More times than not, they have a perspective on you or your product that you can't see. Entrepreneurship creates a special kind of myopia—we are so focused on getting to yes that we miss the other options. Like "Yes . . . but."

If you are truly listening *to learn* and not just listening *to respond*, then you can file that information away and use it to your advantage. The other party isn't gaining information from you, so they don't have anything to use to their advantage. The two of us have put this strategy into practice in business time and again. Listening first before talking works well in politics too.

Next, identify the concrete microgoals for the person across the table from you. When you sit down to do a deal with Target or

Walmart or any big entity, you aren't negotiating with their share-holders, their board, or their CEO. Your fate will be decided by people deep inside the organization. Remember how we said to get through the nos? You need to look at your negotiation in the same way. You need to focus on the priorities that matter to that individual buyer. *What does she need to do to earn her quarterly bonus? What numbers does she have to hit? How can you help? What are the problems your product or service can solve that make a direct difference to that person?* If your company can help her meet her goal, there's a good chance she becomes your champion. Never forget that business *is* personal.

You must always keep in mind the power dynamic when you approach a big customer. But you can push back. Be honest about what it will take for you to work with them. It takes courage to stand up to Goliath—but if you are an entrepreneur, you already have courage. Large companies are not trying to hurt small busi-nesses; they're just trying to manage their own business. Remember that a large corporate executive has likely never run a small busi-ness. You don't get to be a large company executive by running a mom-and-pop shop or struggling to meet payroll. That is not the career path to the C-suite. Fair or not, your experiences are truly academic to most of them, stories they've read in case studies. Thus, they will not be empathetic to or even aware of the challenges of waiting on net 60 payments, securing a loan based on your balance sheet, or ramping up production at five times your normal runtime. You have to make them aware. Be honest. If their practice will hurt your business, don't ignore it for fear of losing the deal. As we said earlier, the cost of doing business should *not* be your business. Play to win, not to avoid losing.

If this feels outside your comfort zone, take heart in the fact that most business owners have not been trained in the fine art of negotiation. Unless they have gone to business school, most people have not studied how to do it and how to do it well. The good news is that as a business owner you'll have lots of opportunities to practice. You are bargaining every day with customers, vendors who sell to you, your landlord, your bank, and others. It's a negotiation when you're trying to get someone to prioritize paying you over other creditors. When you need to buy wholesale and know only what you've got versus how much they want, it's a starting point for haggling—one of the oldest forms of negotiation. Regardless of the circumstances, before you arrive at the negotiating table, understand what you stand to gain and what you could lose and practice getting to what you need.

Like balance sheets and business etiquette, negotiation skills don't dominate public school curricula. Math courses and electives hint at this training, but a student has to seek out this kind of learning, often long before they know they'll need it. As policy makers examine how to help spur entrepreneurship in the U.S., they should look closely at effective ways for business owners to gain soft skills to help them grow, either through Small Business Development Centers, community colleges, or starting in K–12 classrooms.

In the end, most small-business owners today end up learning dealmaking on the job. Those teachable moments can be painful, or worse, threaten the entire business. At the same time, we believe that for small businesses to grow and thrive, they need not only training and mentoring but concrete opportunities to work with large customers.

The real catalyst to igniting growth among small firms is giving them a chance to do more business with large customers and supporting them so they can be successful. While companies including UPS and McDonald's have launched new initiatives to work with small, diverse suppliers, more big corporations and government agencies need to step up too. They must acknowledge that the underlying complication holding many small businesses back is that they are often overlooked, and when they do finally secure a contract, they suffer because they are not paid on time. As our friend Susan Sobbott, the former American Express executive who ran the credit card company's small-business division, underscored to us, commerce—the flow of buying and selling—is what builds skills in entrepreneurs and drives small firms to implement the discipline and sophisticated systems they need to survive and thrive. When a large corporation or government agency buys from a small business, they give that entrepreneur something in addition to revenue that is priceless: they give them the ability to put all they have been taught into practice and to build the processes and policies that will help them grow more sustainably. Access to commerce leads to longevity.

Scaling Now

Our experiences getting to know Terrez and building a portfolio of large corporate Now partners, including Coke, MBDA, Intuit, and others, continued to help Now grow and reach all types of small-business owners. By September 2013, the demand for NowAccount was picking up speed as we served clients in nine states with YTD revenues of $100,000. In June, July, and August alone, we processed $4.6 million of payments that we financed with $5 million from our lines of credit from credit unions. We expected to reach breakeven by the end of the year. But we could not keep growing at this fast clip if we continued to fund the business by piecing together $1 million to $3 million lines of credit at a time. Not only was the process time-consuming, there was a cap on what we could borrow from the credit unions. They are limited by law to loaning only 12.25 percent of their assets, and we needed much more to scale. After much thought, weighing whether to raise more equity or borrow from a bank, we finally decided to secure a $15 million line of credit from Virgo Investment Group, a private-equity firm, which would allow us to accelerate more payments to our clients.

Our story and the creative way we underwrote and financed Now caught the attention of Harvard Business School. Researchers wrote a case study of our unique funding decisions that has become part of the entrepreneurial finance syllabus. Lara travels to Cambridge every fall to help lead the students in discussion when the case is taught. As she explains to them, each dollar Now pays out to our clients is a dollar we borrow (at a lower cost than our clients could borrow). We had created a way for small businesses to get their revenue immediately without them having to borrow money to keep cash flowing, because Now was doing the borrowing and shouldered the risk. Soon our little fintech would be mature enough for us to start financing the company by selling our own bonds on the U.S. bond market. We had grown to forty employees and were finally breaking even. But soon enough we would see once again why there is no finish line in business. Another fire to put out or a new opportunity to chase is always right around the corner.

LEVEL-UP LESSONS: CHAPTER 10

- Understand the power dynamic of large corporations. The fact that a senior executive gets you in the door does not mean you have a customer. In large corporations, there is no one person who can say yes, but there are lots of people who can say no. Your goal is to get through the nos.

- When trying to secure a customer, show the customer why they need you instead of trying to sell your product or service. The presentation should be about them, not about you. Sell your impact.

- Look under the hood of a big customer for opportunities in their supply chain. Many small businesses set their sights on the Goliath customers and run out of money trying to catch them. Serving Goliath's suppliers is a great way to level up with less risk.

- Negotiations can be scary, but don't go into them with the mindset that one side has to lose in order for the other side to gain something. Focus on how to grow the pie for all. Figure out where each party's assumptions differ and create a scenario in which each party benefits if their assumptions turn out to be true.

- Always look to change the game. If the game is designed to work against you, change it. If you are a small business who competes with larger competitors on price, offer extended terms and change the game. Be honest about what works for you and what doesn't, and don't be afraid to push back.

It became routine for us to get a call or email from one of our clients asking us to introduce them to someone in our network. There was the guy whose firm made concrete-block molds who wanted to know if we knew of any good marketing firms. Or the two Black women founders who were looking to pair up with another minority-owned business to bid on a government contract. Just as many small businesses are invisible to the public because their work happens behind the scenes and along the supply chain, we saw that they are often hidden from one another too. The more matches we made, the more we felt a little like old-time switchboard telephone operators making connections one by one. Always thinking about optimizing our time, we decided to try to make some of these introductions all at once in the same room.

We invited several dozen Atlanta clients to join us for a meet and greet on a Wednesday evening in May in Now's new office space, the funky former home of an antique-map and book shop. We carefully curated a guest list that would maximize the networking potential. After arriving, guests clipped on name tags while we consulted a notebook that tracked who needed to meet whom, then walked them over to say hello. Over wine and platters of cheese and crackers from Costco, the room buzzed with lively conversation as they got to know one another and exchanged business cards. It was so much fun to see everyone from an IT services company to an architect interacting. We connected an 8(a) certified cybersecurity company looking to serve more hospitals with a client who provided financial technology solutions to hospitals. We knew firsthand how lonely entrepreneurship can be and how hard it can be for a

11

. . .

THROUGH THICK
AND THIN

One of the joys of building Now that we never saw co
was the chance to play matchmaker. No, we weren'
ting up CEOs on blind dates. We were informally con
ting intrepid business owners to one another so they could buy f
and sell to one another and, better yet, partner to go after la
contracts. By the spring of 2016, Now was serving several hund
small and midsize firms that ran the gamut from manufacturers
maple syrup to screen cleaners to landscapers, from staffing
IT, from marketing and PR firms to companies building pow
substations—just about any business you could think of. And the
were all hungry for contacts.

small business to find and vet the right partners and customers. We had learned through Terrez and her work with Coke that a smart way for smaller and newer companies to generate revenue is to find work with other small and medium-size firms or to team up on big contracts. We were gratified to play a role in helping our clients help one another and to get to know them even better. The Now happy hours became a monthly event and would plant the seed for a new phase of the company down the road.

We felt unstoppable. Not only were we expanding the company's scope and our ability to support small businesses in multiple ways, we were setting new goals for revenue and clients and checking them off one by one. With the 2016 election season off and running, Stacey's political commitments continued to swell. People outside Georgia had begun learning of her after the 2014 legislative cycle and the launch of her nonprofit to register marginalized voters, the New Georgia Project. State house races in Georgia and national contests began reaching out to her. In the summer, the 2016 Democratic National Convention in Philadelphia featured her as a speaker, and later, she crossed the South speaking to thousands of Hillary Clinton supporters at campaign rallies. As Lara continued to grow Now into the profitable business we envisioned, Stacey was pulled more and more toward her passion for politics and civic engagement, but this time we had the staff and resources to support and replace our different roles. Our partnership had always been based on honesty and doing what called us. It wasn't a surprise that we were heading for another crossroads.

Friends (and Cofounders) Forever

Even though we both were busier than ever, we still found a way to squeeze in our teatime tradition. On a warm May afternoon in 2016, we sat at a table for two in the Candler Park district in east Atlanta. Dainty origami birds and colorful paper lanterns dangled above our heads as we sampled the buttery scones and sipped herbal tea at a bohemian shop called Dr. Bombay's Underwater Tea Party. Not only were we celebrating Lara's birthday, we toasted being together for the first time in too long.

Lara regaled Stacey with the growing pains of a staff that now exceed twenty employees. Ever the team builder, Lara had instituted activities to keep the team motivated and connected. Some of Now's earliest employees had come into their own and were taking on more leadership responsibilities, with mixed results. More clients had joined the roster, and more partners had agreed to work with Now's clientele. The company had matured, and unlike Nourish, its trajectory seemed assured. We spared a moment of nostalgia for Nourish, which Stacey was in the process of formally dissolving. Our massive, expensive mold had long ago been moved into a storage facility, and we mused about what potential resale value it had (none, it turns out). Final K-1s were being prepared for our shareholders, and all creditors had been resolved.

Inevitably, though, talk turned to Stacey's future with the company. We both knew that managing the New Georgia Project and leading the Democratic Caucus had become the central fulcrums for her. She acknowledged that her value-add to Now had become less fundamental. As we had throughout our work together, we returned inevitably to the question of where her presence was *essential*, versus where she was *important*. We agreed she was certainly important to Now, but we had put together a terrific team and Stacey had been integral in making sure her responsibilities were covered. She told Lara she thought she should tender her resignation, a poignant but practical decision. While the business could thrive without Stacey's day-to-day involvement, her political and civic work could not.

The decision also reflected one of our basic rules for working together: we never wanted Now to become politicized. We had come so far and created so much by devoting ourselves to advocating for small businesses of all types and using our ideological differences and unique points of view to think differently about solving problems. We had always believed that empowering entrepreneurs was neither a blue nor a red issue. With Stacey's rising profile, it would become increasingly difficult for Now to remain apolitical in the public eye. But instead of being forced into a choice, we anticipated the threat and sought to diffuse it.

As our tea cooled, we reminisced about what we'd accomplished in a decade: from wearing waders in a frigid Alaska river to unloading Nourish bottles at a college football game to tag-teaming a skeptical investor about our solution to the dreaded net 30. Passing each other at the airport as Lara headed to California to woo a credit union and Stacey headed to Wisconsin to cajole a development authority into trying out our payment system. We had been through so much together, and we would miss seeing each other as often. Stacey promised she would be there as an adviser and always be a phone call or text away. She wouldn't step away immediately, but by the end of our tea, we knew her departure was right around the corner.

By Election Day 2016, Stacey had formally left the company to pursue her calling to public service. In the meantime, Now sped toward fully deploying the $15 million line we had received from the private-equity firm headed up by a serial entrepreneur in Silicon Valley, as well as the additional lines we had secured from credit unions on our way to successfully issuing our first bonds, which would put us in a position to scale exponentially with practically limitless capital. We needed to reach a significant scale to access the bond market, and the banks wanted either a large amount of equity on our balance sheet or capital from a sophisticated VC or private-equity firm (in debt or equity) to give them comfort. We were finally hitting the moment of lift that we thought would take us to the next stage of scale. All our plans, of course, hinged on trust in our clients. We believed we had vetted them thoroughly and that our internal systems and processes continued to manage both scale and risk.

We never could have predicted that one of our clients had quietly begun to prey on a human weakness and would nearly take us down.

Stuff Happens

The first red flags began to go up in 2016, when we noticed payments that were supposed to be sent to Now from our client's customers were not arriving in our account as they had been. We discovered that our client, a woman-owned construction business in the Midwest, was intercepting payments rather than remitting them to Now, per our agreement. At first, our staff thought it was an innocent mistake. Maybe the customer had not yet updated the address in the payer's system. It was possible that if we were dealing with a large corporation or government agency with lots of bureaucracy there might be a delay. We notified our client and they rectified it while we put additional protocols in place. In early 2019, our new CFO, Amelia DiVenere, was pulling together materials for our annual audit and noticed some concerning discrepancies. The operations team and our former CFO, who had retired, insisted there was no way that there could be an issue with this client given the additional safeguards that had been put in place. To our horror, Amelia ultimately uncovered that our client had indeed stolen money from us. The timing could not have been worse, as our credit facility with Virgo was maturing in a matter of months and we would have to pay back the $15 million in full.

If we defaulted, it would be game over. We would lose the entire company, our clients would lose the use of NowAccount, which they had come to rely on, our teammates who were like family to us would lose their jobs, and our friends and family investors would lose their investments. As it turns out, the Virgo fund was about to close and return capital to its investors. Our failure could also hurt them. The ripple effect was staggering.

Never, Ever Quit

Suddenly, the startup we had birthed, that had been through so much and was getting ready to scale, was facing death at the hands of a single bad actor. Lara felt incredibly alone. She was dying to share this shocking turn of events with the one person who could really understand the depth of her fear, anger, and dismay, even though she had not been involved in the day-to-day operations of Now for more than two years.

Stacey picked up her phone as soon as Lara's number popped up and listened patiently as Lara told her the story and finally broke down in tears of frustration. Lara explained that, while it was still unclear that there was actually a problem (several folks in the company thought it was a reporting issue), she was going to be on the first flight to San Francisco the next day to meet with Virgo and share her concerns. In Stacey's characteristic level-headed way, she urged Lara to take a deep breath. She knew Lara well enough to know that despite the dire situation, Lara would never give up. As different as we are from each other, this is one attribute we share. In your darkest hour, you never quit. You take a deep breath and power on, you lean on the inner circle of your network for strength, and you think outside yourself. You don't only solve your own problem, you look beyond it to a solution that prevents it from happening to others who come after you.

Stacey was speaking from recent experience. She had spent 2018 locked in a highly publicized and contentious battle to become the governor of Georgia (it would have made her the first Black woman chief executive in the nation). In the midst of her Democratic primary campaign, Stacey's opponent, former state representative Stacey Evans, tried to weaponize Now and took aim at her ability to collaborate with Republicans. Luckily, because we had always operated with transparency and were fully aware that questions would come, Lara and John Hayes easily rebutted accusations against the company. Stacey could point to her earlier disclosures to her GOP rivals, and while they certainly opposed her run, they validated her integrity in operation. In the end, the race did not go her way and she did not concede. But in the wake of the painful defeat, Stacey did not quit. Not by a long shot. Instead, she launched Fair Fight Action, a national nonprofit that advocates for the protection of voting rights across America.

Just as Stacey emerged from the 2018 election and started Fair Fight, so Lara would emerge from the overwhelming despair of being victimized by a client and resolve to build a stronger company. Failure was not an option, and in the process we would protect other businesses from future risk.

Own It

Lara felt strongly that the situation had to be handled in person with Virgo, even though other team members dismissed the urgency of a meeting. We both agreed that the seriousness warranted an honest face-to-face discussion. It was the only course. No matter what the outcome, or how hard it would be, the only way to deal with this crisis was to own up to it as soon as possible, make no excuses, and be brutally honest. One of the hidden forces that can ruin a business is treating relationships as purely transactional. But as we have underlined throughout this book, we believe that all business *is* personal, whether it's between you and your partners, your customers, your suppliers, or your lenders. When you enter into an agreement with anyone, you bring your whole self, not just your "business" self. The weight of your word has to mean something. Without integrity, you have nothing.

This conviction is what gave Lara strength as she headed for the airport to fly to San Francisco, along with Marc Adelson, Now's new chief operating officer and chief credit officer. It felt like the longest flight she had ever taken. They would break the news to Jesse Watson, Virgo's founder and chief investment officer, and hope there was a way to salvage Now. Lara, who is typically never at a loss for words, didn't know what she was going to say. She'd only met Jesse for ten minutes a couple of times and didn't really know him or his temperament at all.

Eight hours later, she swallowed hard as their Uber from SFO pulled up to a beige three-story office in a suburb in the heart of Silicon Valley. Once inside, she was shown into a glass-encased conference room with a long table. There was Jesse, a sandy-haired, youthful-looking executive, seated at the far end. As she took a seat, Lara started off the only way she knew how. She apologized.

"I am so sorry, but I think we have a big problem. I don't know how big it is yet. I hope I am wrong. But I wanted to tell you. I don't want there to be a surprise. There is a chance we cannot pay you back when this note matures," she told him solemnly.

Jesse didn't scowl or raise his voice. He gently asked Lara to walk him through her concerns. She explained how and when the issues were spotted, and how she and the team were trying to figure out what they had missed. When she finished, she looked Jesse in the eye and said he could go ahead and foreclose on the company and just take the keys, but she would find a way to make it right. She admitted that she had no idea what it would take, but she wouldn't quit unless he wanted her to step down. If she was part of the problem, she would own that and resign.

Jesse had started several companies himself before founding his firm in 2009 and was no stranger to the ups and downs of entrepreneurship. He listened intently and finally responded, "Well, let's dig in. Let's figure out if this is isolated or systemic. Let me get my guys to help you do some analysis and go through the numbers."

Many of us have been taught that apologizing shows weakness. We are always amazed at the number of entrepreneurs who will lead with ego and defend their approach even when mistakes and flaws are evident. When you are in a defensive posture, you are not listening. If you're not listening, you can't learn and improve. You are destined to repeat the same mistakes. We believe that when something does not go the way you had hoped, you should start with "I'm sorry" or "My apologies." Own up to your mistakes and ask for input. It worked for Lara and saved Now.

Jesse told Lara that he wanted to help because Lara was forthcoming and transparent and he felt certain she wouldn't give up until it was fixed. We had always believed that the way you operate in life is the same way you should operate in business. There was no other way Lara could have approached this situation except to be completely candid and open about the failings. We saw in action that at the end of the day, all you ever really have is your word. In business, trust is everything. Jesse believed that too. And because he trusted Lara and her leadership, he was rooting for us.

Keep Calm and Carry On

Starting that afternoon in California, Lara began to plot out how we were going to come back from the brink.

She and Marc raced back to Atlanta and got to work. Through more analysis, our team confirmed that the theft was an isolated incident. There was no systemic issue. It wasn't that our whole business model didn't work. It appeared that human error and overly complex, manual processes obscured the theft for too long. We would have to make some changes, but it was fixable. That was the good news. The bad news was that we still owed Virgo the money, and despite pursuing legal remedies to recover our losses, the process dragged on.

Soon Jesse came back to us with a possible way forward, but it would sting. Virgo would convert some of the outstanding debt to equity and his firm would take a major stake in our company. Virgo would also invest additional equity capital to enable us to scale. The eleventh-hour infusion of capital would save us, most of our employees, and shareholders, but it would come at a high price to family and friends who had invested in Now early on. The value of their shares would be diluted. They would have a chance to put in more cash to retain more ownership, but you can imagine how frustrated and angry they were to learn that their investment was worth a fraction of what they had invested. This included the two of us. We had both invested our own money into Now (not to mention our blood, sweat, and tears), and on paper, our investments would nearly be wiped out. But we both knew this was the right way forward for everyone. Lara called each and every investor, spoke on the phone with some and met others in person, to deliver the news.

Growth Mindset

Jesse told us that he felt Now was an even better investment than some new startup with a similar idea *because* we had stumbled. We knew where the landmines were and wouldn't make the same mistakes again. That's why he was betting on us. Recapitalization meant we would be giving up a lot, but never for a second did we think we shouldn't do it. We focused less on what it meant for us and more on the truth that failure is not an option. This was always much bigger than us. We knew our clients needed us and our employees had worked hard and deserved to be part of the company's ultimate success, so we could not fail them. Our investors put money into this, and whether it would take three years or thirty years, we were determined to earn them a return on their investment.

As an entrepreneur, you sometimes feel like you are carrying everything on your shoulders and that you can't possibly afford to stumble. Messing up is never an easy thing to admit, but we know it can be especially fraught for entrepreneurs who don't fit the mold. If you are a white male founder and you make a mistake, it's often treated as a dress rehearsal, and you're given the chance to try again. Failure is almost seen as a badge of honor. The capital markets let you try again. The regulatory markets let you try again. Often your customers will let you try again. But we know it's often the opposite when you are a marginalized or disadvantaged business owner.

Instead of being a dress rehearsal, a stumble is a death knell. One mistake is seen as *a predictor* instead of *a practice run*. You lose access to capital, you lose access to marketplaces, you lose access to customers. You're not given a chance to make another mistake. Whatever your weaknesses, you're not given the opportunity to shore them up.

You can't control bias all alone, but you can control how you react to adversity. We cannot underscore enough that the forces that hold small business back are *both* external and internal. You must know the difference and keep reminding yourself what is in your power, so you can meet the moment.

Take a Step Back

In business, there is no such thing as uninterrupted success. You have to be ready to execute when things don't go as planned. Jesse likes to say that entrepreneurs are always "dancing between the raindrops." It's not easy to stay positive when there is so much uncertainty and anything can happen. But that's the job.

No one likes to step back and look at things that don't work out because it forces you to experience the stress and the emotions all over again. But it also allows you to be a bit more objective than you were when you first went through it. You will see signs you missed that you will be able to identify next time. Perhaps the greatest benefit of stepping back and analyzing what went wrong is realizing that you survived. The confidence and resilience that you develop from a success is fleeting, but the grit and belief in yourself that you develop from recovering from a failure is lasting. Working through our challenges made Lara realize that she has a level of resilience she never knew she had. She realized that she was able to pick up the pieces and keep moving, even on her worst days, and that she was strong enough to get through anything and come back even stronger.

In the spring of 2020, after spending the better part of a year working with Jesse on restructuring the company and on a game plan for our short-term financing, Lara had planned to gather the board and shareholders at our offices to unveil the next steps. It was a moment of high anxiety but also of hope and optimism that we could right the ship and hold on to all we had built, both as a payment solution for our small-business clients and as an increasingly vocal advocate on their behalf. But within days of the big meeting, yet another bombshell dropped, something none of us had seen coming. And this one was completely out of our control. COVID-19 had locked down the nation and the world.

LEVEL-UP LESSONS: CHAPTER 11

- Partnerships that stand the test of time will see each partner's role change over time. Great partnerships flex to fit changing life circumstances and new opportunities.

- Stuff happens. How you respond to problems defines your future.

- Be honest. Admit mistakes. Apologize. Own it. ALWAYS.

- Step back and analyze what went wrong. Often when we experience a failure, we are so quick to vacate the premises that we never look back. Force yourself to look at what happened from all angles. You will realize that there are not only great lessons to be learned, but that the same misstep can't take you down again if you own it.

12

THE FUTURE IS NOW

The pandemic disrupted plans, rearranged lives, and threatened the economy on an epic scale. For Now, while we too were surprised by the onslaught, we were ready for it. The theft had been a stress test, and the internal changes we instituted fortified the company. Before COVID-19 arrived, we had already turned more attention to digital marketing and solidified our risk management systems and processes. With Virgo's investment, we were able to secure bond capital, which further insulated us during the economic downturn. We had weathered the tumult and persisted, even thinking bigger with Jesse's encouragement. Jesse challenged us to build an "Olympic" team of talent to take us to the next level and to "think beyond payments." The big meeting in our offices with our board and investors, planned for March 2020, at which Lara was to unveil the changes and the new plan for the future of Now, had to be scrapped and switched to Zoom. From her dining-room table, Lara guided Now's biggest stakeholders through the changes ahead, calmly fielding questions. Jesse had planned to fly to Atlanta to rally the troops, but that would have to wait.

Fail Fast. Fail Forward.

On March 13, 2020, the team had begun working remotely, indefinitely. For Lara, it was especially hard going through this emotional and cultural challenge without being in the same room with the team, the board, or the investors. Everybody was scared, and it had nothing to do with Now. They feared for their health, their relatives, and their kids, who weren't in school. But the team at Now had already survived so much, and they persevered. As the economy shut down, Lara still put on a brave face and moved ahead with plans to raise more outside funding.

She drew inspiration from a sailing trip she had taken during business school. As a person who gets carsick in a New York City taxi, she had been armed with every motion-sickness remedy on the market. At one point, the sailboat crossed a channel of rough water, and the captain asked everyone to secure loose items and prepare for "some bumpiness." As they navigated the channel, the "bumps" got larger and larger and sometimes even crashed over the deck of the boat. Everyone held on, and Lara kept glancing back at Captain Ron, who was standing steady at the helm, whistling, smiling, and guiding the boat through the channel. He did not seem nervous, and this comforted her. When they reached calmer waters, Lara asked Captain Ron if the channel was usually this turbulent, because the bumps had seemed pretty big. With a slight grin but earnest eyes, Captain Ron replied, "It does no good for the captain of the ship to stop smiling."

Lara was now the captain of the ship, and she had to keep a steady course: the team, the clients, and the investors were looking to her to gauge the situation. She needed to keep smiling. You need to keep smiling too, when your business hits unexpected difficulties. And it will. But don't ever forget that you set the tone for your team. If you want them to remain calm and confident, you must convey it. There will always be factors out of your control, but *how* you lead through troubled times is determined by you.

Our company needed even more money to grow at the rate Virgo expected if we were going to get to the other side of the crisis. We were fortunate to have the capital from the bond structure, a funding source we'd set up using a variation on the securitization conversation we'd had with John Hayes all those years ago. We back-stopped our transactions with municipal bonds, a novel approach that proved stable when others in our space had their capital pulled or reduced. As a result, we ensured that we could continue to accelerate payments to our clients. Because of the pandemic, their cash-flow needs had never been greater. Expanding our infrastructure would require millions more. Lara found herself once again rehearsing her talking points and polishing Now's pitch deck. Instead of flying out to the Bay Area to woo investors, she would have to persuade them to bet on Now's future via the stilted format of video conference. With Virgo on our side, Jesse's connections, and

Lara's steadfast ability to trigger her network for new prospects, her calendar filled up with Zoom invites. Even beyond the remote format, this was a markedly different experience than the one we had while trying to raise investment in Nourish, when our pitching had fallen flat. Suffice it to say, we had been down this road before, and even if she didn't let it show, Lara was feeling the pressure.

VC Isn't for Everyone

One of the most important lessons we learned going through the arduous and disappointing process of trying to raise private investment in Nourish is the extent to which small businesses assume they *have to* raise venture capital or they won't be taken seriously. Venture capital is not the right fit for every company. It should only be used when the nature of your business requires it to grow exponentially in a short amount of time. Ironically, entrepreneurs have been conditioned to think all businesses should do that, which is unfortunate, because most of the businesses we rely on every day grew slowly and steadily over decades. Think Johnson & Johnson. The Walt Disney Company. General Motors.

While many small-business owners say access to capital is one of their biggest worries, and lack of it certainly was the death knell for Nourish, more money isn't always the answer to a company crisis. As we've cautioned, you have to consider the source and the cost. When you agree to take funding from private investors, you give away some portion of ownership or equity in your business, and that means a loss of control. You have poured in your time, your energy, your intellectual capital, and not a few relationships building this startup. Are you ready to let other people tell you how to run it?

Venture investors will now have a say in your operations, and may even displace you if they feel it's time for a change in leadership. They will expect returns on a timetable. While VCs invest in long-term growth potential, they will expect you to scale fast and put pressure on your company to expand quickly and produce very large returns. If your business is not structured to create meteoric value in a three-to-five-year time frame, then it will likely be the wrong match for investors and destined to fail. A sudden big infusion of capital can also create unforeseen headaches and temptations. You may feel pressured to throw money at expensive new hires, fancy office space, and lots of PR that add window dressing but no real value. You confront choices you likely wouldn't have budgeted for when you were bootstrapping and still counting every penny. Choices made from leanness tend to harden your company's resilience. Choices born of excess lead to ballooning expenses and burn through the very cash you should be conserving for the basics. On the other side, you won't be judged on other's expectations but on *your* decisions. So choose wisely.

We share this with you because otherwise you risk raising outside money and ignoring the most important part of your business—growing and sustaining *revenue*. Slow and steady growth is not sexy. It's not usually how startups are portrayed on TV and in the movies. Instead, fresh-faced tech founders who raise tens of millions of dollars on an idea alone are glorified, plastered on magazine covers, and pitched softball questions instead of tough ones from the press. The very worst of this culture anoints emperors (or empresses) with no clothes, those charismatic founders who earn breathless media coverage without any real evidence that their business fundamentals support the accolades and multibillion-dollar valuations. Think Adam Neumann of WeWork, Elizabeth Holmes of Theranos. The ethos of "fake it till you make it" runs rampant through Silicon Valley, where "success" is based on the amount of money a brash entrepreneur can raise simply on the promise of building a profitable business and on the perceived value—not necessarily the real revenue.

"You don't read about the woman or the man who started the dry-cleaning business and built twenty-five dry cleaners and is a multimillionaire. Everybody hears about the Silicon Valley wunderkind who at the age of twenty-four is worth a billion dollars because they raised three hundred million from Andreessen Horowitz," observes our friend Karen Robinson, a serial entrepreneur who advises and invests in early-stage companies.

Karen knows both sides of the coin. When she raised $41 million in private equity as CEO of Enrev, a cutting-edge battery-charging business, she was hailed as one of the first female entrepreneurs in the Southeast ever to raise such an eye-popping sum. For a long time, it was all people wanted to talk about when they met her, even though the money was all on paper. And once she raised all that money, she felt compelled to keep raising more.

"I allowed myself to get caught up in it. Financing becomes an end, not a means. All of a sudden, it's almost like a bad drug addiction. You were so addicted to raising capital that you'd spend all your time raising capital instead of trying to build a good business," she told us, looking back. Enrev was planning to IPO at a $1.1 billion valuation, but the offering was postponed due to market conditions. The company was later sold.

Not long after, Karen was brought on as CEO of an outdoor advertising firm and took a completely different approach to growing the business. The company raised very little institutional investment, and instead Karen put the focus on figuring out how to expand profit margins. The business sold ad space on telephone booths, and Karen decided to invest in figuring out how to microtarget the ads to specific groups of customers in different neighborhoods. This was in the days before everyone had a mobile phone and when the idea of geolocation was still futuristic. She and her team used census data to develop their own mapping software that could show how specific telephone booths would reach the most relevant customers to advertisers.

At the same time, the business began looking more closely at the demographics of the actual ad buyers for outdoor placements and discovered that many of them were young men and women in entry-level positions. The new mapping tool could make their tedious jobs much easier and efficient by bundling dozens of locations for ads so the young buyers could perform faster. Remember how we said to sell the impact of your product or service? This is a prime example. Karen observes that neither of these revelations would have happened if she was devoting all her time to raising outside funding. The solution to spurring revenue came from looking under the hood of the actual business and identifying smart ways to do things differently. In the end, Karen grew annual revenue by 50 percent, pushed operating profit margins to 55 percent, and led the company to profitability in three years. The business was sold in 2006 for a twenty times return.

Ask the Right Questions

With our plans for rapid growth in the near future and our track record, we felt Now would be attractive to outside investors. As a fintech, we were not bogged down by supplies, equipment, or physical inventory, which meant we could scale faster than we ever could have scaled Nourish. We felt comfortable parting with some of our ownership in order to fuel our new fast track. If you think VC is the right avenue for your business, it's important to understand the timing, dynamics, and what you should expect from the relationship. The right investors can be critical when your values and goals are in alignment. But you need to examine this up front. Karen encourages entrepreneurs to interview investors just as seriously as they are interviewing you. *What are the milestones your business will be expected to meet and how is the investor positioned to help you get there? What happens if you miss the mark? And what skills, contacts, and coaching can they bring to your team and your board that will fill knowledge gaps in your company?*

As COVID-19 hit and bottlenecks slowed down supply chains, Helya Mohammadian was relieved that the lead investor in her company, Slick Chicks, could offer insights from her own deep experience managing suppliers. When Helya discovered a shipping issue with one of the new big-box retailers selling her products, the investor, Michele Gay, CEO of the cosmetics company LimeLife by Alcone, even met her at Slick Chick's New York warehouse to help investigate the problem. For Helya, the support and encouragement has become invaluable to her business's ability to scale, and as she looks ahead to fundraising in the future, she believes the investor relationship transcends capital alone.

"We are in constant communication. She's my biggest cheerleader," says Helya of Michele Gay, adding that it is also important for a founder to be able to be vulnerable with their investors and ask for help.

In addition to the rapport you will build with investors, you want to understand in detail where your company fits into their investment portfolio and the life of a fund. Will your startup be the first investment in a fund or the last? And what is the life span of the fund? This is important, because the earlier you are in a fund, the more time your company will receive to meet benchmarks and the more time investors can spend coaching and helping to guide your growth. You will need to clarify what the obligation to your company will be if or when the fund closes. *Will your company be sold to another group of investors so that you will have to answer to a new team that may not share your goals?*

There is also the matter of how you and your management team will be compensated if or when your company ultimately has a "liquidity event," meaning the shareholders get a payout because the business has been acquired or goes public. It may seem far away, but you need to comprehend how your share of the equity is structured, so that you walk away with compensation that is fair and not diluted so much that you aren't left with what you think you deserve.

Do your homework. Reach out to the founders of other companies in the investor's portfolio to learn about their experiences and how investors treated them in difficult times. Speak with the board members of other portfolio companies and ask about the dynamics in board meetings. Try to talk with companies in the portfolio that have been successful and those that have not. Check out the diversity of the portfolio and of the investment firm. If the portfolio isn't listed on the firm's website, look them up on Crunchbase and see who they've funded, at what level, and at what stage. Talk to other investors and entrepreneurs who may know the firm or managing partners. VC is a tiny world, and if you start digging, you are bound to find someone who has experience with a particular firm, investor, or partner. Follow them on social media. Set news alerts on Google so you are aware when the investor or fund has announced a new investment.

"Understand who you're targeting, who you're talking to . . . and make sure this is someone that you really want to be close with over the life of your company. . . . You need to sit down and say, 'If I get X dollars from this company and it cost me Y percentage, how can I demonstrate and can I articulate how my company will be better off?'" says Karen. Entering into a relationship with private investors will have a lasting impact on the trajectory of your company. In other words, you need to live with it, so make sure you have all the facts *before* you sign the term sheet.

As Lara continued fundraising, she was also thinking of growing and evolving Now's board to reflect the needs of the company. She was looking for someone with a stronger IT background, someone with strong sales and marketing chops, and someone with procurement experience. People often think they report to the board, but in fact the board works for the company as well. So you need a board that will work not only to provide governance but to provide value in their respective areas of expertise.

Grow Fearlessly

One of the reasons for expanding the skillsets of our board was that Jesse and Lara had begun to talk about how to scale Now beyond payments. It was time to innovate and think of how else the company could make a bigger impact. This was an exciting and daunting prospect. Growth is inherently uncomfortable and scary. But you have to embrace it or you'll never evolve. Lara knew this from experience. She would have to face the unknown if she was going to seek out new directions for the business. Looking around the fintech space, it was clear that our competitors were focused on offering more types of financing solutions. *But what if we could do something to help small businesses actually do more business?*

As it turns out, Lara already had an idea in her back pocket. She told Jesse about the Now happy hours and how it seemed that Now's clients were craving a way to find one another, as well as to finesse introductions to big corporate and government procurement offices. COVID-19 had thrown a wrench into everyone's business, challenging their supply chains, their access to capital, their health and wellness, their ability to find employees, or even their ability to simply remain open. The worst economic downturn since the Great Depression made connections to customers even more critical. Lara told Jesse about clients like Kevin Mobley, who owned an industrial engineering company, the Ian Thomas Group, and was looking to be introduced to firms that might want to buy large orders of protective face masks for employees; Andrea Burnett of Power House Pest Control, who wanted to find more customers interested in contactless inspections; and Greg Allen, who owned Superior Products Coatings, which sold a type of specialized coating to protect against heat transfer, and was hoping for an introduction to Procter & Gamble. Even if our clients couldn't meet new customers face-to-face, we had continued to facilitate fertile connections for them. At the same time, procurement officers had started coming to us asking for referrals. Seeing these efforts bear fruit underscored our belief that the natural supply chain of money to small businesses is by selling stuff, not by borrowing money from banks or other lenders. If 99 cents of every dollar that goes into your company comes from your customer paying you revenue, then the best way to grow your business is to get more revenue.

Lara explained her big idea to Jesse: What if Now could build its own platform that didn't just connect buyers and sellers but would curate who should talk to whom? It would be a marketplace powered by artificial intelligence and an algorithm that could make the best and most useful connections depending on what our clients and corporate partners needed.

In Lara's mind, if we could get you a customer faster so that you could deliver faster, then we could get you revenue faster, and we've created a flywheel of growth. It would put our formula of customers + commerce = capital into practice. What we would call the NowNetwork could create a new and different way to position small businesses for success. This prescription could be especially potent for historically disadvantaged business owners at a time when they were in the spotlight.

The outcry over the death of George Floyd turned attention to the injustices of systemic racism in America and the structures that have blocked access to economic opportunity, education, and health care for communities of color for generations. Small businesses suffered terribly during the pandemic, especially BIPOC-and women-owned companies, which, as we mentioned, missed out on the first round of federal aid when lockdowns began, and policy makers were taking notice. African Americans experienced the largest losses: a 41 percent drop in the number of active business owners. Latinx businesses also faced major losses: 32 percent. Immigrant business owners suffered a 36 percent drop, and female business owners 25 percent. Small-business advocates like Victor Hwang and his organization, Right to Start, were lobbying government procurement offices at the federal, state, and local levels to commit to shifting 5 percent of their spending from big corporations to minority suppliers. Blue-chip companies like PepsiCo, Apple, and PayPal unveiled new multimillion-dollar equity and inclusion initiatives and pledges to contract with more diverse firms.

We felt our new NowNetwork could help big companies and government agencies more easily and fluidly identify small and marginalized firms while providing a new avenue for business owners to do more new business. The Now clients were already vetted, because they were using our payment processing and had gone through an exhaustive review of their capacity. Our partners viewed it as a kind of "Good Housekeeping Seal of Approval" that would certify a small firm's ability to handle a contract, whether it was a hundred-thousand-dollar job or a million-dollar opportunity. Lara began to put together an advisory board to work on an initiative that would bring large corporate partners to the table. We would be bold in our efforts to open up a whole new frontier for the company.

Launch a Movement

The launch of a new division of Now was yet another pivot anchored in our desire to help level the playing field for small businesses so they can stand the test of time. What began as our unlikely journey to figure out how to earn a living on our own unexpectedly veered into a manufacturing venture, then a heartbreaking master class on the cash-flow woes of small businesses. This inspired our fintech, a fresh perspective on trade credit and corporate America, and the chance to forge relationships with hundreds of entrepreneurs who inspire us with their perseverance. From our new vantage point, we could look out and see the scope of what we could achieve if we leveraged all that we had learned to unite and empower these enterprising individuals. As we met people like Alisa Clark of Glory Professional Cleaning Services, who would become one of our clients and use Now to grow her company into a multimillion-dollar firm and one of the largest corporate maintenance businesses in the Southeast; and Sheila Jordan, who used the cash flow from Now to build her transit content as a service software without having to raise a dollar of private investment or borrow from a bank; and Traci Morgan, the food and beverage engineer, who can take on multiple contracts from some of the biggest consumer-products giants that have ninety- to one hundred-twenty-day payment terms with the confidence that she can pay her team on time, we knew that in our next chapter our mission would be even bigger. We wanted to start a movement. Small business has always been the backbone of the U.S. economy, the leading job creator, and a driver of both innovation and economic promise. Owning a business has the power to transform families and entire communities. But as we have shown and learned ourselves, these enterprises have become increasingly fragile, and they need to be nurtured. It is time for small-business owners to regain our footing in America and come together to help one another level up.

With access to capital and commerce, we can do it. We call on policy makers to address the structural barriers that make it tough on business owners to scale and sustain their enterprises. It is time for regulators to examine the capital markets and the restrictions on credit that make it so expensive and difficult for entrepreneurs to borrow. We need the SBA to redefine the way it identifies small businesses so that it reflects the diversity of firms and their unique challenges. We need the public education system to offer training in financial literacy, business finance, and entrepreneurship, as well as technological skills like ecommerce, data analytics, web design, and social media content creation. We need to ensure that all communities have access to reliable, fast internet and the ability to access modern technology equipment so they can compete. We need you to know that you are not alone. The future is now if small businesses reach out to one another, share knowledge, and tackle opportunities together.

Homecoming

As the idea for the Now Network began to take shape, Lara could barely contain her excitement. In the spring of 2021, she called Stacey to share the latest plans and asked if she would consider coming back to Now as a member of a new advisory board overseeing the Now Network. Stacey had been busy since leaving Now and her gubernatorial campaign. She'd founded three organizations to focus on voting rights and public policy and had experienced a trial by fire in the 2020 elections. A record number of voters turned out in the contentious 2020 U.S. presidential election in Georgia and in hotly contested runoffs for the state's two U.S. Senate seats. Democrats prevailed in all three races, but Stacey's focus had been broader than simply winning elections.

Fair Fight Action, the voter protection nonprofit she'd founded, faced off against attacks on voting rights across the country. As state legislatures attempted to roll back voter protections, Stacey drew on her partnership with Lara and constantly reminded anyone who would listen that defending voting rights was a nonpartisan endeavor—that she could be an unabashed Democrat, but she was an American citizen first. On top of the work of Fair Fight, her census organization, Fair Count, was hard at work ensuring that the 2020 Census yielded positive outcomes for hard-to-reach populations: people of color, the poor, young people, and the marginalized. She'd also launched a third organization, the Southern Economic Advancement Project, which focused on an equitable economic recovery for Southern states ravaged by the COVID-19 pandemic.

In addition, she was preparing for the much-anticipated publication of her legal thriller and a new venture—Sage Works Productions, Inc., a production company that used her Selena Montgomery novels and nonfiction books as intellectual property for television and film. To put it mildly, Stacey was busy. And yet, when Lara told her about the next phase of Now, she readily agreed. The renewal of our fifteen-year partnership was the best kind of homecoming. We knew that relationships and roles could change and flex to fit our complex lives. For Lara, Connor was now in high school, and Casey had expanded his business vision. We had come a long way from a lunch line at a leadership conference.

Where you fit into an organization can evolve, but the underlying obligations of friendship and fealty do not. Regardless of whether Stacey was a compensated employee, a stockholder, or just a friend who believes in the business, she was going to be at the table. Because she believes in Lara. And Lara knew she could ask, because the feeling is entirely mutual.

In the months ahead, Lara would continue to pitch investors, and in June 2021, the two of us headlined the Zoom press tour announcing Now's $9.5 million new round of funding led by Virgo and Cresset Capital Partners. A month or so later, we finally got a chance to really visit for the first time in close to two years.

Thunder and rain raged outside Lara's home as Stacey knocked on the front door. The house was new, but when she was ushered inside, the destination felt familiar—Lara's kitchen. Because of the pandemic, we hadn't been able to meet face-to-face. But Lara had made a birthday gift for Stacey, knowing we would get together when it was finally safe again. As soon as we saw each other, we hugged, and then Lara brought out a rose-and-lavender-framed picture of a tea set she had painted herself.

Stacey marveled at the perfect gift and said quizzically, "I didn't know you painted."

"I don't," Lara replied. "I'm just getting started. But I wanted you to have my first one."

"I'm in," Stacey answered, secretly musing there was probably a business plan hidden inside the frame.

A chance to solve a new puzzle, to conquer a new horizon. A chance to level up—again. And that is as it should be.

LEVEL-UP LESSONS: CHAPTER 12

- You are the captain of the ship. Keep smiling.

- Think outside VC. Venture capital works for some, but there's no shame in not being the kind of business that VCs want.

- Do your homework on investors. Ask them for references. Ask them for examples of successes and failures and what they would have done differently or what they did to contribute to their success.

- While policy makers need to address the systemic forces that keep small businesses from accessing capital, commerce, and coaching, business owners can help one another change the game: Buy from one another. Collaborate on deals. Share knowledge and contacts. Be vulnerable about challenges and mistakes. Raise your voices to draw attention to structural weaknesses. Together, we can level up NOW.

To find out more and join the
Level Up movement:

ACKNOWLEDGMENTS

STACEY ABRAMS

Sustaining the pursuit of a business ambition demands all manner of investment—definitely financial capital, but less often lauded, copious amounts of patience, forbearance, and forgiveness. I appreciate these coming in abundance from those named and unnamed, including (in alphabetical order) Jeanine Abrams McLean, Kathy Betty, Lisa M. Borders, Genny Castillo, Reena Wyatt Cherry and Byron Cherry, David Cofrin and Christine Tryba-Cofrin, Edie Cofrin, Shannon Cofrin Gaggero, Johnnetta B. Cole, Rebecca DeHart, Will Dobson and Kelly Cole, Brandon Evans, Shirley Franklin, Sarah Beth Gehl, Greg Giornelli, Lauren Groh-Wargo, Carolyn Hugley, Archie Jones, Allegra Lawrence-Hardy, Eliza Leighton, Dara Lindenbaum, Roger Merrit, Steve Phillips and Susan Sandler, Ashley Robinson, Morgan Smith, Darnell Strom and UTA, Donald Sussman, Carol Tolan, Don and Ellen Walker and the Harry Walker team, Teresa Wynn Roseborough, and

Pai-Ling Yin. I also offer appreciation to John Hayes, a relentless believer that better is out there.

With constant gratitude to Linda Loewenthal, my phenomenal agent; agent Lisa Leshne, who deftly represented this project; and the extraordinary Portfolio team: Adrian Zackheim, Niki Papadopoulos, Kimberly Meilun, and our intrepid guide, Merry Sun. Thank you to my amazing team of jugglers and fencers: Samantha Slosberg, Michael Holloman, and Mandisa Surpris.

And with a debt of affection and appreciation to my magnificent coauthors: the prodigious Heather Cabot, who captured our voices and our stories—without losing either; and my ever–business partner and true friend, the brilliant Lara O'Connor Hodgson, who sees around corners, through walls, and beyond the horizon to a future brighter than we can fathom alone.

LARA HODGSON

There is no greater falsehood about business than "It's not personal." Nothing is more personal than working with other people toward a greater goal. It takes vision to see what others cannot, stubbornness to believe when common sense supports the contrary, grit and determination to pursue a path against the raging current of the way things have always been done, and empathy to care enough to create something for the benefit of others. No person can do this alone and so it is with undying gratitude that I acknowledge the following individuals and so many more that are listed in my heart even if not on this page for never letting me give up and for never giving up on me: Ms. Klister and my St. Pius X High School family, who told me I had a right brain; Gary May and my fellow Georgia Tech Giants, who demanded that leadership does not come with personal accolades or gravitas; George Williams, who taught me to ask for help; Katherine White, who taught me the importance of people; Bill Sahlman and my friends at Harvard Business School, who opened my mind to entrepreneurship and allowed me to pay it forward; Sarah and Bob Bua, Joe and Wendy Kahn, Susan, and Jon Levine, who made Boston a real home; Bert Ellis, who bet on me twice; Bill Nussey, who was the best boss I will ever have; Tom Shields, Frank Bishop, and Stewart Long, who reminded me that in challenging times the quietest action will always speak louder than a megaphone of words; Jodi and Glen Weintraub and Genevieve and Remco Bos, who have picked me up more times than I can count; John Hayes, who is a gifted inventor; Monsignor Richard Lopez, who sets the bar for making the world a better place that I will always strive to meet; my dear mom friends Blake, Tracey, Jacqueline, April, Lisa, Sara, Mara, and Susan, who are my village; Jesse Watson, Ed Weisiger, and Kyle Limberg, who believed in me when I did not; Marc, Sejal, Earl, Sarah, Mel, Amelia, Rebecca, Bertaud, Alexis, Raja, Paulina, Mayra, Amanda, Betty, Brenda, David, Joey, Carmella, Cindy, Ashley, Alex, Tabish, and all who were part of or will be part of the Now Team, who serve small businesses tirelessly; Jim Reinhart and Max Scherr, who have helped me Level Up; Kelly Dwyer, who is my professional coach and an amazing mirror (If you don't have a coach, get one!); my fellow EY Winning Women, who redefine success and significance; and each and every client, partner, lender, or investor who has supported our efforts to enable businesses to grow fearlessly.

I would not be on this adventure if it were not for the incredibly talented Lisa Leshne and The Leshne Agency, who encouraged us to share our story and who have shepherded this book from idea to print. The opportunity to meet and work with Heather Cabot, an amazing writer, mom, and now, friend, who truly has a gift for finding the nugget that makes us realize that we are extraordinary, one and all, is truly a blessing. The Portfolio team led by Adrian Zackheim, Nikki

Papadopoulos, Kimberly Meilun, and Merry Sun is unparalleled in both vision and in execution.

There are no words to express the impact that Stacey Abrams has had on my life as my business partner and my friend. A friend is someone who gives you the freedom to be yourself, is one of the most valuable things you can have, and is the best thing you can be. Thank you, Stacey, for being the best and for enabling me to be my best.

HEATHER CABOT

I want to express my deepest gratitude, admiration, and affection for Stacey and Lara and their phenomenal teams. Thank you for welcoming me into the Atlanta fold with warmth and good humor. Thank you for trusting me with your inspiring story and for treating this project like a true team effort. Thank you to my dear friend and literary agent Lisa Leshne of The Leshne Agency, who spearheaded this book and believed in me. Thanks to attorney Candice Cook Simmons for your wise counsel and sunny encouragement. To editor Merry Sun, you personify grace under pressure. I am so grateful for your thoughtful feedback and, especially, on deadline. Thank you to Niki Papadopoulos, Adrian Zackheim, Jane Cavolina, Kimberly Meilun, and the entire Portfolio family for your support and enthusiasm. To my best friend and life partner, Neeraj Khemlani, who lifts me up every day and makes me a better person and storyteller; our amazing children, Ian and Sam, who inspire us with their curiosity, wit, kindness, and smarts; my wonderful parents and mother-in-law; Cabot and Khemlani sibs, nieces, and nephews; our huge extended family across the globe; and our beautiful circle of friends in Rye and around the country, thank you. Please know I could not do this work without you. Thank you for always cheering me on and helping me reach for the stars.

NOTES

CHAPTER 1: UNLIKELY BUSINESS PARTNERS

1 **during the recovery:** Leigh Buchanan, "American Entrepreneurship Is Actually Vanishing. Here's Why," *Inc.*, May 2015, https://www.inc.com /magazine/201505/leigh-buchanan/the-vanishing-startups-in-decline.html.

2 **half of new businesses:** Karen G. Mills and Annie Dang, "Creating 'Smart' Policy to Promote Entrepreneurship and Innovation," National Bureau of Economic Research, NBER.org, May 19, 2020, 1, https://www.nber.org /system/files/chapters/c14508/c14508.pdf.

2 **high-tech, high-growth tech startups:** Mills and Dang, "Creating 'Smart' Policy to Promote Entrepreneurship and Innovation," 4.

3 **denied bank loans:** Robert W. Fairlie, PhD, and Alicia M. Robb, PhD, "Disparities in Capital Access Between Minority and Non-Minority-Owned Businesses: The Troubling Reality of Capital Limitations for MBEs," U.S. Department of Commerce, Minority Business Development Agency, January 2010, 3, https://archive.mbda.gov/sites/mbda.gov/files/migrated/files-attach ments/DisparitiesinCapitalAccessReport.pdf.

3 **women-owned ventures:** "21st Century Barriers to Women's Entrepreneurship," Majority Committee Report of the U.S. Senate Committee on Small Business and Entrepreneurship, July 23, 2014, 2, https://www.sbc.sen

ate.gov/public/_cache/files/3/f/3f954386-f16b-48d2-86ad-698a75e33cc4/F7
4C2CA266014842F8A3D86C3AB619BA.21st-century-barriers-to-women
-s-entrepreneurship-revised-ed.-v.1.pdf.

4 **disparities between Black and white wealth:** Patricia Cohen, "Beyond
Pandemic's Upheaval, a Racial Wealth Gap Endures," *New York Times*, April 9,
2021, updated April 12, 2021, https://www.nytimes.com/2021/04/09/business
/economy/racial-wealth-gap.html.

4 **This critical fumble:** Anne Sraders, "Black-Owned Small Businesses Face
Hurdles Even as COVID Eases and Optimism Rises," *Fortune,* June 8, 2021,
https://fortune.com/2021/06/18/black-owned-small-businesses-obstacles
-inequity-post-covid-recovery-small-business.

4 **Only 12 percent of Black and Latino business owners:** "Federal Stimulus
Survey Findings," Global Strategy Group for Color of Change and Unidos
US, May 2020, 3, https://www.unidosus.org/wp-content/uploads/2021/07
/UnidosUS-Color-Of-Change-Federal-Simulus-Survey-Findings.pdf.

4 **83 percent of entrepreneurs:** Victor Hwang, Sameeksha Desai, and Ross
Baird, "Access to Capital for Entrepreneurs: Removing Barriers," Ewing
Marion Kauffman Foundation, April 2019, 1, https://www.kauffman.org/wp
-content/uploads/2020/06/Access-To-Capital_2019.pdf.

5 **$1.2 trillion of trade credit:** Ramana Nanda, William A. Sahlman, and
Lauren Barley, "NOWaccount," Harvard Business School, case study 9-814-
048, October 2013, revised, August 11, 2016, 6, https://www.hbs.edu/faculty
/Pages/item.aspx?num=45837.

7 **greatest engine of job creation:** John C. Haltiwanger, Ron S. Jarmin, and
Javier Miranda, "Who Creates Jobs? Small vs. Large vs. Young," U.S. Census
Bureau Center for Economic Studies, paper no. CES-WP-10-17, August 1,
2010, https://papers.ssrn.com/sol3/papers.cfm?abstract_id=1666157.

7 **America's thirty million:** Mills and Dang, "Creating 'Smart' Policy to Promote Entrepreneurship and Innovation," 3.

13 **Eighty-one percent of small businesses:** Mills and Dang, "Creating 'Smart'
Policy to Promote Entrepreneurship and Innovation," 3.

13 **the highest number of Americans:** "New Business Formation in America
Goes Bezonkers," *Economist,* June 26, 2021, https://www.economist.com/united
-states/2021/06/26/new-business-formation-in-america-goes-bezonkers.

13 **a record number:** John C. Haltiwanger, "Entrepreneurship During the COVID-19 Pandemic: Evidence from the Business Formation Statistics," National Bureau of Economic Research, NBER Working Papers Series, June 2021, 1, https://www.nber.org/system/files/working_papers/w28912/w28912.pdf.

14 **The 24.3 percent surge:** "Megaphone of Main Street," Small Business Report presented by SCORE, U.S. Small Business Administration, Fall 2021, 16, https://s3.amazonaws.com/mentoring.redesign/s3fs-public/Fall%202021%20Megaphone%20of%20Main%20Street%20Small%20Business%20Jobs%20Report%20FINAL_0.pdf.

14 **drew a stark contrast:** Haltiwanger, "Entrepreneurship During the COVID-19 Pandemic."

CHAPTER 2: WATCH OUT FOR GRIZZLIES

31 **women raised less than 2.2 percent:** Joanna Glasner, "Something Ventured: Despite Blockbuster Venture Investment, Female Founders' Share of VC Funding Falls," Crunchbase News, September 21, 2021, https://news.crunchbase.com/news/something-ventured-blockbuster-venture-investment-female-founders-funding-falls.

32 **the story of Interface Carpets:** Interface Carpets, "Our History," Interface.com, https://www.interface.com/US/en-US/sustainability/our-history-en_US.

CHAPTER 3: IT'S NOT WHAT YOU KNOW. IT'S WHAT YOU NOTICE.

37 **A 2020 Kauffman Foundation:** Sameeksha Desai and Travis Howe, "Who Doesn't Start a Business in America? A Look at Pre-Entrepreneurship Leavers," Ewing Marion Kauffman Foundation, November 2020, 11, https://www.kauffman.org/wp-content/uploads/2020/12/Who-Doesnt-Start-A-Business-in-America-November-2020.pdf.

39 **Sara started selling Spanx:** Video transcript, "How Spanx Got Started," *Inc.*, January 20, 2011, https://www.inc.com/sara-blakely/how-sara-blakley-started-spanx.html.

40 **Surrounded by thick forest:** "About Us," English Mountain Spring Water Company website, https://englishmountainh2o.com/about-us.

46 **"a two-tiered system"**: Bruce Katz, Della Clark, and Colin Higgins, "The Virus and the City: Can Philly Perfect PPP?," *Philadelphia Citizen*, December 22, 2020, https://thephiladelphiacitizen.org/can-philly-perfect-ppp.

47 **With these efforts, Pennsylvania improved**: Telephone interview with Bruce Katz, director, Nowak Metro Finance Lab, Drexel University, August 6, 2021.

CHAPTER 4: CUSTOMERS + COMMERCE = CAPITAL

63 **Black business owners start companies**: Robert Fairlie, Alicia Robb, and David Robinson, "Black and White: Access to Capital Among Minority-Owned Startups," Stanford Institute for Economic Policy Research, Working Paper 17-003, February 2017, https://siepr.stanford.edu/research/publications/black-and-white-access-capital-among-minority-owned-startups; "Start Us Up Now: America's New Business Plan," Ewing Marion Kauffman Foundation, 16, https://www.startusupnow.org/wp-content/uploads/sites/12/2021/03/AmericasNewBusinessPlan.pdf.

CHAPTER 5: HIRE PATIENCE. HIRE PATIENTLY.

79 **only twelve hundred of the thirty thousand**: Telephone interview with Della Clark, president, Enterprise Center, August 23, 2021.

79 **one in five U.S. small businesses**: Jessica Looze, Sameeksha Desai, Sarah Steller, "How Quickly Do New Employer Businesses Hire?," Entrepreneurship Issue Brief, no. 3, Ewing Marion Kauffman Foundation, March 20, 2020, https://www.kauffman.org/wp-content/uploads/2021/07/Kauffman_Issue-Brief_How-Quickly-Do-New-Employer-Businesses-Hire_2020.pdf.

79 **Business owners unequivocally ranked**: Telephone interview with John Dearie, President, Center for American Entrepreneurship, August 23, 2021.

79 **Two thirds of small firms**: "Megaphone of Main Street," Small Business Report presented by SCORE, U.S. Small Business Administration, Fall 2021, 5, https://s3.amazonaws.com/mentoring.redesign/s3fs-public/Fall%202021%20Megaphone%20of%20Main%20Street%20Small%20Business%20Jobs%20Report%20FINAL_0.pdf.

80 **"It is incredibly lonely":** Telephone interview with John Dearie, August 23, 2021.

80 **It's the brainchild:** Abbianca Makoni, "Tech Icon Arlan Hamilton Has Launched a New Start-Up Called HireRunner," People of Color in Tech, https://peopleofcolorintech.com/business/tech-icon-arlan-hamilton-has -launched-a-new-start-up-called-hirerunner-heres-what-we-know-so-far/?utm _source=rss&utm_medium=rss&utm_campaign=tech-icon-arlan-hamilton -has-launched-a-new-start-up-called-hirerunner-heres-what-we-know-so-far.

CHAPTER 7: GROWING OUT OF BUSINESS

108 **Capital Purchase Program:** Rebel A. Cole, "How Did the Financial Crisis Affect Small Business Lending in the United States?," DePaul University, for SBA Office of Advocacy, November 2012, i, https://www.microbiz.org /wp-content/uploads/2014/04/SBA-SmallBizLending-and-FiscalCrisis.pdf.

108 **dropped by 18 percent:** Cole, "How Did the Financial Crisis Affect Small Business Lending in the United States?," 2.

108 **make less risky loans:** Karen Gordon Mills and Brayden McCarthy, "The State of Small Business Lending: Innovation and Technology and the Impli- cations for Regulation," Harvard Business School, Working Paper 17-042, 2016, 19, https://www.hbs.edu/ris/Publication%20Files/17-042_30393d52-3c61 -41cb-a78a-ebbe3e040e55.pdf.

111 **Federal Reserve report found:** Board of Governors of the Federal Reserve System, "Access to Financial Services Matters to Small Businesses," *Consumer and Community Context* 1, no. 2, November 2019, https://www.federalreserve.gov /publications/2019-november-consumer-community-context.htm.

118 **likely as female founders:** Susan Coleman and Alicia Robb, "Access to Capital by High-Growth Women-Owned Businesses," National Women's Business Council, April 3, 2014, 81, https://cdn.www.nwbc.gov/wp-content /uploads/2018/02/27191226/High-Growth-Women-Owned-Businesses -Access-to-Capital-Report.pdf.

118 **2.6 percent of VC:** Courtney Connley, "Black and Latinx Founders Have Received Just 2.6% of VC Funding So Far in 2020, According to New Re- port," CNBC, October 8, 2020, https://www.cnbc.com/2020/10/07/black

-and-latinx-founders-have-received-just-2point6percent-of-vc-funding
-in-2020-so-far.html.

CHAPTER 8: LEVEL UP NOW

126 **64 percent of the small businesses:** Ramana Nanda, William A. Sahlman, and Lauren Barley, "NOWaccount," Harvard Business School, case study 9-814-048, October 2013, revised August 11, 2016, 2, https://www.hbs.edu/faculty/Pages/item.aspx?num=45837.

127 **more than a third of small businesses:** Erin Griffin, "Why Startups Fail, According to Their Founders," *Fortune*, September 25, 2014, https://fortune.com/2014/09/25/why-startups-fail-according-to-their-founders.

129 **small and medium-size business sellers:** Nanda, Sahlman, and Barley, "NOWaccount," 6.

132 **retailers funded more credit:** "The Impact of Credit Cards on Small Business," Hearings before the House Select Committee on Small Business, 91st Congress (Washington, DC: U.S. Government Printing Office, 1970), 364, https://books.google.com/books?id=oVMtAAAAMAAJ&pg=PA360&lpg=PA360&dq=open+book+retail+credit&source=bl&ots=kF_FFQel_6&sig=ACfU3U2ALMWgDfhGQ_WufGZE64CKzKbj8Q&hl=en&sa=X&ved=2ahUKEwipx7mG483zAhXmZzzABHZMsCeQQ6AF6BAgPEAM#v=onepage&q&f=false.

132 **first all-purpose credit card:** Joseph Nocera, "The Day the Credit Card Was Born," *Washington Post*, November 4, 1994, https://www.washingtonpost.com/archive/lifestyle/magazine/1994/11/04/the-day-the-credit-card-was-born/d42da27b-0437-4a67-b753-bf9b440ad6dc.

133 **most consumer credit:** "Quarterly Report on Household Debt and Credit," Federal Reserve Bank of New York, Center for Microeconomic Data, August 2021, 4, https://www.newyorkfed.org/medialibrary/interactives/householdcredit/data/pdf/HHDC_2021Q2.pdf.

CHAPTER 9: KNOW YOUR NUMBERS

154 **"Financial literacy among entrepreneurs":** John Dearie, President, Center for American Entrepreneurship, email interview, September 14, 2021.

154 **SCORE webinars can offer free help:** Alisa Clark's experience with an unhelpful SCORE mentor was the exception.

CHAPTER 10: THE BIG BAD WOLF

173 **companies including UPS and McDonald's:** Alexis Bateman, Ashley Barrington, and Katie Date, "Why You Need a Supplier Diversity Program," *Harvard Business Review*, August 17, 2020, https://hbr.org/2020/08/why-you-need-a-supplier-diversity-program; Hilary Russ, "McDonald's to Boost Diversity Among Suppliers 25%," Reuters, July 22, 2021, https://www.reuters.com/business/sustainable-business/mcdonalds-boost-diversity-among-suppliers-25-2021-07-22.

173 **By September 2013:** Ramana Nanda, William A. Sahlman, and Lauren Barley, "NOWaccount," Harvard Business School, case study 9-814-048, October 2013, revised, August 11, 2016, 13, https://www.hbs.edu/faculty/Pages/item.aspx?num=45837.

CHAPTER 11: THROUGH THICK AND THIN

179 **New Georgia Project:** Stacey Abrams, *Minority Leader: How to Lead from the Outside and Make Real Change* (New York: Henry Holt and Company, 2018), 54.

CHAPTER 12: THE FUTURE IS NOW

205 **41 percent drop:** Robert Fairlie, "COVID-19, Small Business Owners, and Racial Inequality," National Bureau of Economic Research, *The Reporter*, no. 4, December 2020, https://www.nber.org/reporter/2020number4/covid-19-small-business-owners-and-racial-inequality.

205 **PepsiCo, Apple, and PayPal:** Gayle Markovitz and Samantha Sault, "What Global Corporations Are Doing to Fight Systemic Racism?," World Economic Forum, June 24, 2020, https://www.weforum.org/agenda/2020/06/companies-fighting-systemic-racism-business-community-black-lives-matter.